Rootstown United
Church of Chrest

Floral Decorations
for your Church

Christmas, Stanford Memorial Church, Stanford University, Calif.

Floral Decorations
for your Church

FERN BOWERS HUNT

CHILTON COMPANY—BOOK DIVISION
PUBLISHERS   PHILADELPHIA, NEW YORK

Published in Philadelphia by Chilton Company,
and simultaneously in Toronto, Canada, by Ambassador Books, Ltd.

LIBRARY OF CONGRESS CATALOG CARD NUMBER 60–8094

MANUFACTURED IN THE UNITED STATES OF AMERICA
BY QUINN & BODEN COMPANY, INC., RAHWAY, N. J.

FOR MY FAMILY

Ernest Paul Hunt
Pauline Hunt Bell
Victor Richard Bell
Marjorie Hunt Ridgway
Whitman Ridgway
Richard Bell
Steven Bell
Carolyn Bell
Marjorie Manning
Katherine Manning
Opal Bowers Phillips
James Bowers
Della Bowers Burnham
Gifford Bowers

Foreword

It is difficult to imagine a person in love without a gift of flowers to the beloved. The Christian faith is essentially an affair of the heart. Its gospel is the proclamation of the God Who loves us. It is the experience of being so loved by Him. Nor is this just a "spiritual" experience of God. His love of us is not without signs and symbols. Indeed, by the Sacraments, God vouchsafes the gifts of His love, His Spirit, and His Christ. In response, ours would be an answering love of Him. Without flowers among other gifts? Scarcely!

The altar stands for God. As our children are instructed, so do we need a refresher course as children who would love the Father.

Q. What does the altar say to us?
A. The altar says, God is here.

Q. What does the cross say to us?
A. The cross says, God loves us.

Q. What do our flowers say?
A. Our flowers say, We love you, O God.

Flowers do say that, or should. They may, however, declare just as forcibly, if carelessly plunked into a vase, that we do not love Him very much.

Just as a group of faithful women ministered unto our Lord in the days of His flesh, so may faithful women of an altar guild know a direct satisfaction from doing something directly unto Him. To study, to learn the techniques of arrangement, to select the finest flowers,

vii

and to place them as a love offering unto God in His house are rare moments of great privilege. Each of us needs some work of our hands to express the love of our hearts.

I gladly write the Foreword for this book, not as a pastor of a great church which would give distinction to the work of Fern Bowers Hunt, for neither I nor the church I serve is so qualified. Rather, ours is a very small church. A few years ago it would have been classified as a country church. But it did have an altar. Slowly we were able to change from a "decorating committee" into an altar guild. To the invitation to study, to learn, to work at the very heart of the church's mission—to worship and to glorify God—a group of faithful women gathered. It has been an inspiring group with which to work. In its eagerness to make the finest offering unto God, the first fruits of our abilities to show our love of Him, our group engaged Mrs. Hunt as a consultant. We have been further blessed by her willingness to offer a series of classes each year for our members. The artistry of the floral offerings that have graced our worship of God has given its own inspiration to our congregation as well as a greater glory to God. The commendation of this Foreword is a most practical one. If it has been done in our church, with all its limitations, it can be done anywhere. And the one who has been so helpful to us can give that same help in your Macedonia by means of this book.

Churches well established in the use of and care for an altar will find valuable help in this work. Pastors of such churches will have been waiting for it. I write in hope that pastors of other churches without a current practice, such as ours of a few years ago, will recognize a need for this volume. I know it will be most helpful in making your church come alive with meaning, and the procession to its altar a more vital experience, the office of your laity as a priesthood of believers a more joyful office. "Then will we go unto the altar of God, even unto thee, O God, our highest joy!"

J. Hood Snavely, Pastor
The Woodside Village Church
Woodside, California

Preface

An arranger wishing to achieve a unified and harmonious relationship between floral decorations and church should devote special attention to historical background. One should recognize a particular architectural style and learn something about its development. It is well also to know what influences were brought to bear on its style from previous eras. No one era stands alone but is linked to those that have gone before. Its art is the sum total of a people's impressions, past and present, expressed aesthetically and honestly. Each epoch has its own conditions—social, economic, and religious—and must be considered according to time, environment, and materials used. From all these traditions can grow fresh and vivid expressions of one's inspirations; one need not lean too heavily on the past but can seek new ideas adaptable to present needs. These conceptions we have learned from Christian architecture. The builders borrowed from the past, even from pagan architecture, when it suited their needs and aspirations.

No art portrays more vividly, aesthetically, or honestly the true feelings, aspirations, longings, and sacrifices of a people than do the church art and architecture of the Early Christians. Epitomized in stone and mortar are their abiding faith and hope for spiritual expression at a time in history when there were wars, discomforts, pestilence, and famine. As a result, the most magnificent church architecture in the world's history grew out of human longing.

Nearly all our present-day churches are adapted from one of the following types—

Early Christian
Byzantine
Romanesque
Gothic
Renaissance

and it is noteworthy that we have physical proof of their authenticity, since most examples given in this book, except the Early Christian types, are in a fair state of preservation. The sublime edifices of ancient and medieval times have provided a guide for today's church architecture. The pointed and semicircular arched openings, peaked roofs, stone pillars, pinnacles, bell towers, spires, brilliant stained glass windows, high vaulted ceilings, long naves, semicircular apses, mosaic and fresco decorations are features commonly found in many of our churches of both traditional and contemporary types. It is these hybrid churches we floral arrangers are asked to decorate. May each act as a challenge to us, offer new horizons, bring fresh inspiration and teach us the real joy of beautifying God's house to His glorification and the edification of the congregations who view our handiwork. Each can be a rich storehouse of inspiration to the perceptive arranger who seeks to unify the floral decorations with the particular style of architecture, furnishing and order of service. This requires careful consideration of its thoughtful plan and its high degree of craftsmanship, whether contemporary or traditional.

FERN BOWERS HUNT

Acknowledgments

My cordial thanks are extended to Rear Admiral (Ret.) and Mrs. Ransom K. Davis for encouraging the writing of this book; to Carol Hartley, whose untiring help and interest helped it to completion; to Emma Gelders Stern, Lucia Pierson Vaughn, Marie Mudra and Lillian Mund, whose help and advice were invaluable; to Dr. Nathan Bowers, Dr. Graham Stuart, Mr. Charles Beardsley, Jessie Whittern, Kathleen Fitz-Gerald, Ruth Stevens and Ruth Aherns for advice; to the Right Reverend and Mrs. Noel Porter, President and Mrs. Wallace Sterling of Stanford University, Chaplain R. M. Minto, Chaplain John Terril, Dr. Elton Trueblood, Reverend J. Hood Snavely, Reverend John Cox and Reverend Marvin Stuart for inspiration; to Mrs. William Kinley Jones, Mrs. N. B. Johannsen, Mrs. Theodore Morehouse, Mrs. Roy Folger, Mrs. Glen S. Warner, Elizabeth Gamble, Mr. and Mrs. Donald Windbigler, Mr. and Mrs. John E. Carr, Mrs. Harry Carr, Mr. and Mrs. James Quinby, Mr. and Mrs. Paul Houseman, Mr. and Mrs. Andrew Cochrane, Mr. and Mrs. Louis Love, Mr. and Mrs. W. B. Owens, Mr. and Mrs. Wells Pleas, Mrs. Dean Buchan, Mr. and Mrs. Carl Wheat, Mrs. Stanley Morsehead, Mrs. Norman Braly, Mrs. George Bliss, Mr. and Mrs. John Burns, Dr. and Mrs. Harold Beaver and my students and other friends for flowers, help, and encouragement.

I am deeply grateful to Lillian Mund, Maude Smith, Ann Scherer, Kathryn Davison, Roberta Pleas, Gwendolyn Hanks, Ruth Munson and Lois Hopper, students, for arrangements, and to William Arborgast, Russell Illig, Berton Crandall and Esther Wagner for photography. To my daughters and my grandchildren for containers, patience and understanding.

F. B. H.

Contents

Floral Decorations
for your Church

✣ 1 ✣

Church Architecture

Early Christian (A.D. 300–900)

The rise of Christianity marks the most significant era of all time. It is a religion based on faith and hope. It originated in Judea and spread westward via Asia Minor, Persia, Greece, and Egypt to Rome. It brought with it customs and traditions from each. At first there were no churches because the Christians were persecuted for their beliefs and hid themselves in caves and the catacombs near Rome, and held their meetings either in these or in homes. In A.D. 313, Constantine, Emperor of Rome, issued the Edict of Milan, giving Christians state protection to worship as they pleased and to build churches. In 325, Constantine embraced Christianity and made it the state religion of the Holy Roman Empire. It then grew in power and spread over Europe and the then known world.

The Christians adapted their first churches after the Roman Hall of Justice (Basilica) because it suited their need for a long nave to hold large congregations and a semicircular, elevated tribunal chamber—a place to set their altar, celebrate their ritual, and seat their clergy apart from the congregation. In these first churches the altar was placed opposite the entrance. This they called the east end, regardless of how the church faced.

The Apostolic Constitution II sets forth an interesting picture of how these early churches were designed, and it helps explain the symbolic meaning of the word "nave," from *navis*, meaning ship, symbolizing Christ. It says: "Let the house of assembly be long in shape

1

and turned toward the East, with its vestries toward the Western end, after the manner of a ship. Let the throne of the Bishop be placed in the midst, and on each side of him let the presbyteria (the elders) sit down, while the deacons stand beside, with closely girt garments, for they are like sailors and managers of a ship. In accordance with their arrangement, let the laity sit on one side with quietness and good order. Let the porters stand on one side and give heed to the men, while the deacons stand at that of the women. Let the deacons watch the multitude and keep them quiet. During the celebration of the Holy Sacrament let the door be watched lest any unbeliever, or one not initiated, come in."

Other characteristics of the early Christian church were its side aisles which flanked the long nave. These aisles were formed by stone piers or columns which had been garnered from the ruins of pagan temples demolished by the Christians. The columns were bridged by keystone arches, post and lintel openings. Floors were of stone or mosaic tile. Walls were straight-sided and constructed of rubble. On the exterior they were faced with plaster and were ornamented on the interior with glass or marble mosaics and with fresco paintings. These decorations depicted angels, martyrs, and scenes from the Bible.

Pope Gregory (the Great) explained these paintings by saying, "Paintings are used in churches, that they who are ignorant of letters at least by seeing may read on the walls what they cannot read in books." Roofs of the early churches were made of timber, but because of the hazard of fire were later replaced with nonflammable materials such as slate. Windows were made small to keep out hot sunrays and bright light. Many of the churches were destroyed or fell into decay and have been rebuilt as many as three and four times.

Examples of Early Christian Churches

Sant Apollinare in Classe Ravenna
S. Clemente, Rome
S. Maria Maggiore, Rome
Basilican Church of St. Peter, Rome
S. Giovanni in Laterano, Rome
S. Paolo fuori le Mura, Rome
S. Apollinare Nuovo, Ravenna
S. Giovanni Evangelista, Ravenna

Early Byzantine (circa A.D. 300–600)

This style derived its name from the ancient city of Byzantium, situated on the Straits of the Bosporus. It later became the capital of the Byzantine or East Roman Empire when Constantine, then Emperor of Rome, embraced Christianity. He renamed it Constantinople in honor of himself. The city of Istanbul now stands on the site.

The art of the Orient permeated the churches around the Black Sea, the Mediterranean, and Asia Minor. It was a mystical and dignified art. Its mosaics and hand-woven materials were richly colorful. The floor plan of these churches was patterned after the Greek cross. The style was adapted to a warm, dry climate. Heavy masonry or brick walls kept the interiors cool, and high, small windows sheltered by an overhang protected the interiors from the bright hot sun. Ceilings were lofty and capped by onion- or melon-shaped domes made of glass mosaic or sometimes feather-light pumice. These rested by pendentive means on a drumlike, central structural compartment which was square, round, or polygon. Triangular segments of building material were placed to fill in between the dome and the compartment and came to rest on sturdy masonry supports. Uncluttered by columns or piers, there was ample space in the center of these churches to hold large congregations.

Walls of Byzantine churches were made of thick rubble or stone faced with native clay or imported marble. Interior walls were often covered with gold-incrusted mosaic tile, showing martyrs and angels, also animals, birds, and flowers in a conventionalized flat manner. Any lifelike appearance in sculpture or painting was strictly forbidden because the clergy feared that seeing it, the people might wish to return to pre-Christian idol worship. Some did, and as a consequence the clergy demanded that every temple and its contents be reduced to rubble. These wishes were never entirely carried out, because Pope Gregory I in a letter to Mellitus, stated: "These temples must not be torn down, but should be put to Christian use. For hard and rough minds it is impossible to cut away abruptly all their old customs, therefore he who wishes to reach the highest place must ascend by steps and not by jumps." He also wrote "that the temples of the Nations ought not to be destroyed, but let the idols that are in them be destroyed; let Holy water be made and sprinkled in the temples; let altars be erected and relics placed."

A distinct difference of opinion between the people of the Eastern half of the Empire and the Western half arose regarding Christ's divinity, the East contending that the Holy Spirit emanated from God alone, while the West declared that the Holy Spirit came from both God and His Son, Jesus. In the year 1054 the Christian Church split apart. The Eastern half became the East Orthodox Church while the Western half of the Empire became Roman Catholic.

Examples of Byzantine Churches

S. Sophia (Hagia), Istanbul
SS. Sergius and Bacchus, Istanbul
S. Irene, Istanbul
S. Theodore, Istanbul
S. Mark, Venice
S. Antonio, Padua
S. Vitale, Ravenna
Church of the Assumption, Moscow
Church of the Gracanica, Serbia

Romanesque (*A.D. 800–1200*)

Romanesque architecture was influenced both by the Roman basilican style and by the Byzantine. It took its name from the Roman. This style spread westward along the trade routes and paths followed by the Crusaders. It was a romantic time in history; King Arthur and his Knights of the Round Table were searching for the Holy Grail.

In rural districts and in small towns the common people formed merchant guilds. They built churches which became their community centers, their places of worship and consolation and education. For the ground plan of their churches they chose the symbolic Latin cross and constructed a long nave (three times as long as wide), crossing it at right angles with a wide transept. At the eastern end they placed a semicircular apse, and opposite it, at the end of the long nave, a narthex above which was set a rose or wheel window. Again, timber roofs were later replaced with slate or similar material. Ceilings were domed and vaulted with transverse arches. Interior walls were magnificently decorated with glass mosaics, marble facings, and fresco paintings. Figures were elongated and conventionalized, expressions lifeless. The various decorative features lacked the refinement found in Byzantine architecture.

Church music during this time was Gregorian. While secular musicians used bagpipes, the lute, violin, and zither, all but the zither were banished from the churches. Even it was allowed to be used only occasionally.

Examples of Romanesque Churches

Pisa Cathedral
S. Antonino, Piacenza
S. Ambrogio, Milan
S. Michele, Lucca
S. Michele, Pavia
Pistoia Cathedral, Pisa
S. Miniato, Florence
S. Zeno Maggiore, Verona
Notre Dame La Grande, Poitiers
Abbaye aux Dames, Caen
Church of the Apostles, Cologne
Worms Cathedral

Gothic

During the 13th, 14th, and 15th centuries, feudalism was replaced by a national government, and during this period Christian people found expression in the stone cathedrals they were building. This type had its birth in France and was copied in Italy, England, Germany, Belgium, Holland, and Spain, but never in its true form. In each country the style differed because of climatic conditions and availability of building materials. Never has an architecture portrayed the thinking of a people more truly than has the Gothic. The pointed arches symbolized hands clasped in prayer beseeching God for deliverance from their miseries. The strong vertical lines reflected aspiration for a better life after death.

Gothic architecture has also been referred to as "frozen music" because of the harmony and unity of its interrelated parts, rhythmic perfection of ribs and vaults, and in its repetition of ornamental detail. This beauty was accomplished because the people of the hamlets where these churches were built tried to secure the services of the very best artisans available to complete their cathedrals. Each cathedral was made large enough to house great multitudes of people and beautiful enough to awe the most sophisticated observers through the centuries. The people claimed that no effort was too great, no gift too fine, for God's house. Entire families, including children, the

FIG. 1. *Grace Cathedral, San Francisco, Calif.* White chrysanthemums arranged in tall silver vases are effectively silhouetted against the deep maroon velvet hangings back of this beautiful High Altar.

aged, even the sick, labored on them, because they believed in heavenly reward commensurate with the time and effort expended.

The Latin cross ground plan was borrowed from the Romanesque style. The nave was increased in width and the walls made much higher so as to make the windows larger and to let in all light possible. The clerestory type of window was used in England; the wheel was not. Thick walls were constructed of small undressed stones set in thick mortar. Roofs were slanted to shed heavy rain. Porches were set in receding stepped-back planes and ornamented with beautiful hand-carved, conventionalized designs showing human figures, plants, and animals in bas-relief. Pinnacles, spires, peaked roofs, and pointed arches emphasized the aspirations of the people. Flying buttresses were also a distinctive feature of this style, as in Notre Dame, Paris.

Late in the Gothic period a new thought in art emerged from the gentle and ardent teachings of St. Francis of Assisi. He taught that it is much better to love and cherish nature than continually to aspire for a reward in Heaven. His thinking was reflected in the church decoration of his time by an increased interest in ornamental window traceries and carvings of plants and animals in natural designs grouped around doorways.

French Gothic (A.D. 1150–1500)

Gothic architecture, cradled in France, was characterized by three different style periods. A fine type of volcanic stone around Caen was available in great quantity for use in building the French cathedrals.

Gothique à Lancettes was an era of pointed arches and geometric window traceries. Beginning at St. Denis, Île de France, it changed from the Romanesque style.

Rayonnant (13th century) was characterized by wheel or rose windows such as seen at Rheims, Amiens, Bourges, Chartres.

Flamboyant (14th century) derives its name from flamelike window traceries. These are seen in the cathedrals at Rouen, Albi, Candebec.

All French cathedrals showed aspiring lines in pinnacles, spires, and transverse arches and diagonal vaulting in ceilings. Naves were short, apses transformed into chevets. Roofs were steep and slate-covered. Porches and doorways were elaborately ornamented. Windows were large and set with stained glass. Sculptured figures were common.

Belgian and Dutch Gothic

Clay was native to these countries, therefore red brick was made from it and used in these cathedrals. Simplicity marked this style, but towers, belfries, and gables of various heights were used. Sculptured figures were placed between door and window openings.

Examples:

Tournai	Ypres
S. Gudule	Notre Dame, Dinant
Antwerp	Haarlem
Bruges	

German Gothic

Cathedrals of the northern latitudes were constructed primarily of stone or from brick made of native clay. Roofs were steep and the same height in both nave and side aisles, differing thus from the French. Ceilings were unusually lofty. Large windows let in all possi-

FIG. 2. *Chapel of Grace, Grace Cathedral, San Francisco, Calif.* White marguerites arranged in gold vases tie in color to the white marble French Gothic mantel, and are subordinate to its exquisite carving and the reredos back of it.

ble light, and these were decorated with branch tracery, a type not seen elsewhere at that time. Another departure from the French type was the western tower which replaced the apse. Entrances were placed on either the north or south side. The ornate sculpture of the recessed doorways was, however, a feature borrowed from the French Gothic. Arches in German churches were not as pointed as in French ones.

Examples:

S. Gereon	Ulm
Cologne	Oppenheim
Nuremberg	Ratisbon
Freiburg	Lubeck
S. Elizabeth, Marburg	S. Stephen, Vienna

Italian Gothic

Great artists congregated in the cities of Venice and Florence, which lay in the path of trade routes and of the Crusades and thus became centers of art and learning. The architecture evolved was characterized by flat roofs, small windows without tracery, a rose or wheel window placed in the east end. Corinthian columns with acanthus-leaf decorations were used to support arches. There was an absence of fresco paintings and pinnacles in this area. Roofs were less steep, if pitched, than those of more northern cathedrals.

Examples:

Milan	S. Petronio, Bologna	S. Francisco, Assisi
Orvieto	S. Maria Novella	Florence Cathedral
Siena		S. Antonio, Padua

English Gothic

English cathedrals were characterized by high stone walls, slate roofs, long narrow naves with few side aisles, ribbed, stellar and fan vaulting. Clerestory windows were much in evidence, as were pointed openings. Curvilinear mullions on windows and perpendicular tracery were distinctions of this country. Aisles were single, steeples tall. Rood screens and sculptured figures were common. Features of the later period typical of England were applied decorations, such as the Tudor rose, bellflower, and dogtooth. Most of the early churches of England were planned and built for monks rather than for lay congregations.

Examples:

Ely	Durham	Canterbury
Norwich	Peterborough	Lichfield
Ripon	Salisbury	Winchester
Rochester	Gloucester	Wells
Exeter	Lincoln	Westminster Abbey

Spanish Gothic

The Gothic cathedrals of Spain reflect the Moorish influence in their domes, horseshoe arches, and semicircular single-span vaults, lacelike window tracery, geometric patterns in mosaics. Walls were thick, windows narrow. There were twin towers on the west end; chevets borrowed from the French replaced the apse. Other distinctive features were screen openwork and choir stalls with intricate carvings. Life-size sculptured figures of angels and martyrs decorated doorways. In the early period, decorations of fruit, flowers, and animals were carved in bas-relief, later to become full relief.

Examples:

Santiago da Compostela	Toledo
Salamanca (Old Cathedral)	Barcelona
	Seville

Renaissance (15th and 16th Centuries)

The term Renaissance means rebirth, a return to Greek classicism in art. The churches of this period were well planned. Most of them had massive, fortress-like stone exteriors and stately interiors. Horizontal lines predominated, as all openings were placed to catch shadows to emphasize the horizontal feeling in design. Post and lintel type of construction was borrowed from the Greeks, as were massive Corinthian columns supporting beautifully decorated domes. Bas-relief carvings featuring the acanthus leaf, egg and dart, and shell decorations were common in the early Renaissance period. Figures in high relief, of beautiful colored marble, were seen in the later Renaissance or Baroque era.

Examples:

Pazzi Chapel, Florence	Church of the Sorbonne, Paris
S. Maria delle Grazie, Milan	S. Mary le Bow, London
S. Maria della Salute, Venice	Valladolid, Spain
Saint Peter's, Rome	Granada, Spain

Spanish Missions (U.S.A.)

The mission churches of our own Southwest and California are monuments to the fearless zeal of the Franciscan friars. They came to the part of America called New Spain to teach their religion to the American Indians and to promote education.

The first mission, San Miguel de Santa Fé, was built in New Mexico about 1600. Like many others, it was destroyed and later rebuilt. The architecture of this and of the chain of California missions along El Camino Real, from San Diego to San Francisco, show a strong Moorish and Spanish Renaissance influence. Plain, solid exteriors were pierced by slitlike windows set deeply in thick adobe or red sandstone walls. Because the interiors are cool and dark, the rich hangings, paintings, and polychrome wood carvings of santos, madonnas, and Biblical characters are, in many instances, in good condition today. Opposite the entrance was placed an elevated altar of rough hand-hewn stone or wood. This harmonized with the sturdy wooden beams or cedar poles that bridged the white plaster ceiling and helped support the heavy roof of sun-baked tile. Above the entrance façade rose the bell towers, and surmounting these, for all to see, stood the Christian emblem of faith and hope—the Latin cross. Surrounding most of the missions ran high, thick walls of stone or adobe to protect the unwary from marauders and the gardens from voracious animals. Inside the walls, and set apart, were the graveyards, mute but grim evidence of the hardships and dangers that beset the brown-robed padres and their congregations.

Mexico and Latin South America

The great cathedrals of Mexico and South America show strong Spanish Renaissance influence in their plain, thick, fortress-like walls and small windows; but the richly ornamented gold-leaf and polychrome carvings seen in the interiors follow after the Gothic style. Onyx is native to Mexico and is used throughout the area for floors and interior furnishings. Despite this, great quantities of imported marble have been used. Most churches are surrounded by heavy stone or adobe brick walls. Chapels are part of this feature, designed to provide space for the overflow of great crowds and to carry on the pageantry which is so essential a part of their religious services.

Examples:

Cathedral of Puebla, Mexico	La Compania Arequipa, Peru
Mexico City Cathedral	San Francisco La Paz, Peru
Cathedral of Cuzco, Peru	

United States (Pre-Revolution)

Early American church architecture is simple and reflects the austere attitudes of the Pilgrims. The first meetinghouses were of rough hand-hewn logs, unembellished within and without. These severe people frowned on all celebrations, including the observance of Christmas. Later, as the colonies grew in number and living conditions became better, the colonists continued to build plain churches but changed from the rough log-type to a distinctive white clapboard style, characterized by vaulted ceilings and a spire or steeple surmounted by an emblem indicative of the denomination. Below the spire was a bell tower. Interiors were simple in design. Windows were long and narrow and of clear glass, the frames painted white. Usually the altar occupied the extreme eastern end of the building and was flanked on either side by choir stalls enclosed in a chancel rail.

United States (Post-Revolution)

Post-Revolution American church architecture followed designs by Palladio, an architect and exponent of Greek classicism. Ceilings were topped by a dome and Corinthian columns supported porticos. All this gave a feeling of dignity and elegance. These churches were usually painted white on both exterior and interior. Beautiful fine-grain mahogany was imported for lecterns, podiums, and pews. Windows were tall and of clear glass. Doors were also tall and usually double.

Rustic

Rustic churches, as the term implies, are usually found in mountain districts or along the wayside in rural areas. They are constructed of native fieldstone, hand-hewn undressed logs, or a combination of the two. In nearly every instance they are harmonious throughout as to textures used and in compatibility with setting. Those the author has seen have peaked roofs, simple altars, and rough benches. Fortunately the people who worship in them are sensitive to their rustic beauty and are eager to keep the fixed and movable decorations

Photo William Arborgast   *Children of the Parish*

FIG. 3. *Episcopal Outdoor Chapel, Lake Tahoe, Calif.* White daisies, simple in form, are effectively arranged in white pottery vases for this rustic mountain setting. These tie harmoniously in color with the candles and linen altar cloths. The cross is made of yellow-green moss and the candlesticks from the white trunks of quaking aspen trees.

simple and appropriate. Field flowers are effectively used for floral decoration, placed in wooden, unglazed pottery or unpolished containers.

Contemporary

Contemporary church architecture reflects the religious, social, and economic development of people living today in a shrunken world—shrunken because of the fantastic advances in methods of transportation and communication. These factors have great bearing on the successful design of the churches of our time. Modern building materials, both synthetic and those of natural origin, are used to great effect. Many of the synthetics are beautiful, long-lasting, easy to handle, and have great tensile strength. By employing these materials and with the aid of precision instruments, power tools, and other

Photo William Arborgast   *Ann Scherer*

FIG. 4. *First Presbyterian Church, Palo Alto, Calif.* Long-keeping white chrysanthemums are set off by the broad leaves of the Bird of Paradise plant. These offer strong
contrast with that of the flowers. The design leads the attention of the observer toward
the foot of the cross in this contemporary style church.

mechanized equipment, enormous and beautiful churches can be built in a relatively short time—short as compared to the years, sometimes centuries, that elapsed in building the cathedrals of the Middle Ages.

Architects today place emphasis on interesting space division and functionalism, and often in tying the interiors with gardens through great expanse of glass. They strive for simplicity in structural features and plan their decorations to grow out of these. In many instances cantilever design is employed. Most people think of contemporary architecture as being severely plain, with flat roofs and a rhythmic placement of moldings, windows, and door openings to give a horizontal line effect. This is true of today's secular architecture, but not so in ecclesiastical design. For builders of churches today still cling to the vertical lines of medieval times, peaked roofs, high vaulted ceilings, tall spires, pointed arched openings, and stained-glass windows that are higher than they are wide.

In essence, the silhouette of the contemporary church differs but little from early predecessors, and it reflects man's thought today as it did then. It would seem that man's spiritual needs have changed little since ancient times; he still looks heavenward in faith and hope for a better life. On the other hand, his physical condition has changed markedly in earthly matters of ease, comfort, and pleasurable living; and he no longer looks to the church building as a literal fortress in time of war. He has learned to harness natural phenomena for his use, learned to span continents and oceans with utmost rapidity so that he might bring the world's great storehouses to his doorstep.

ఊ 2 ఊ

Traditions and Trends in Church
and Secular Floral Decoration

Consider the lilies of the field, how they grow;
they toil not, neither do they spin: . . .
yet . . . Solomon in all his glory was not arrayed
like one of these.

Lilies and other flowers of the Bible have been associated with divine love. They have often been referred to as having a spiritual quality akin to music, poetry, and the sacred psalms of the Old Testament. It is therefore understandable why Pope Gregory (the Great) in his instructions to St. Augustine admonished the clergy to sanction flowers for the church and for the home and to encourage this popular practice.

We know that each country had its own particular style of arrangement. Truly to understand floral arrangement design, we must know how this art was practiced in pre-Christian times, both in the Occidental and Oriental worlds. We have proof in stone carvings, paintings, and illuminated manuscripts that this art paralleled other creative art forms in reflecting the life and thought of the times.

Egypt

The ancient Egyptians living along the banks of the Nile River were fortunate in having both plant materials in abundance and clay and other materials from which to make containers. This perhaps accounts for the unusual number of floral arrangements pictured on stone that have been unearthed in the pyramids and temples along the Nile. The stone carvings show us how floral decoration was practiced as early as 2500 B.C. The arrangements then were as stiff, stylized, and symmetrical as the pyramids and other art forms of that culture. The early Egyptians were an intelligent, artistic people of persevering and unrelenting character. The despot rulers of the country drove their slaves unmercifully to build the massive pyramids which are monuments to the Pharaohs' ambition and pride. The people showed great engineering skill, for it is said that these pyramids of gigantic stone blocks do not deviate more than six inches in symmetrical measurements, according to present-day computations with precision instruments. The Egyptians were also sophisticated gardeners, as an Egyptian poem written more than three thousand years ago testifies:

> The rushes of the garden were verdant
> And all its bushes flourishing.
> There were currant trees and ripe cherries,
>   redder than rubies,
> The ripe peaches resembled bronze . . .
> The garden is today in its glory.

The fact that the women of Egypt were more independent than the women in some other countries of antiquity probably accounts for the practice of self-adornment pictured on stone. They made floral wreaths for head and arm bands, and wove garlands of flowers and leaves to decorate their stone columns and water jars. Wheat, lotus buds and blossoms, papyrus, palm, barley, durra (black millet), crown daisies, grass peas, Egyptian lupin, narcissus, opium poppy, lilies, and flax were among the plants used in arrangements.

Many plants were used symbolically in ceremonies (see Appendix II, Symbolism of Plant Materials). These were placed in vessels of gold, silver, and faience. The lotus (blue or white water lily) was the first to bloom in spring and was used as a harbinger of the coming harvest. During the reign of Ikhnaton, huge arrangements of the lotus being used in religious ceremonies were depicted on stone. The Egyptians combined bright flowers that followed a triadic color scheme, such as yellow, blue, red, black, brown, orange, and green. Surprisingly, these arrangements were pleasing because in hot, dry countries, the shimmering heat waves tend to cause colors to mingle.

Photo Russell Illig   *Fern Bowers Hunt*

Fig. 5. There is a strong sense of motion in the dramatic forms of the Bird of Paradise flowers in this arrangement. These are placed to point in one direction and are ade-
quately supported in visual weight with the broad crisp leaves of the Ti plant. A wood-
form, placed to simulate the waves of an ocean, also suggests a sense of rhythm. This
arrangement would be appropriate for the recreation room in a contemporary type
church or in an Egyptian or Mexican setting.

The Mayas

It is a source of constant interest that we find—across the world
from Egypt—a people, the Mayas, whose arts and culture paralleled
in many ways that of the Egyptians. The Mayas, too, built tombs.
They, too, have left evidence of exquisite flower arrangements im-
mortalized in stone. The modern arrangement of Mexican material
illustrated above in its angular symmetry recaptures a gleam of this
remote and vanished world.

Greece (600–350 B.C.)

This was a glorious age in Greece. Art flourished and reached its
zenith. Architecture, sculpture, and ceramics of this period are un-

equaled as masterpieces of refinement, restraint, and taste. There is little evidence that floral decorations were used to fill their exquisite vases.

These were decorated with garlands of flowers and leaves, as were courtyard pillars and doorways. Garlands and wreaths were also strewn on banquet tables. After the snows on Mount Olympus, Parnassus, and Zeria had melted, a profusion of flowers illumined the fields and filled the market place in Athens. Bards have sung of Greece's Elysian fields.

Flowers used symbolically and for fragrance were roses, acanthus, honeysuckle, cistus (rockrose), cyclamen, violet, lily, cornflower, iris, wild currant, hawthorn, and the leaves of the olive, fig, mulberry, laurel, oak, and maple.

Roman Empire (100 B.C.–A.D. 350)

The Romans borrowed many customs and designs from the Greeks, among them the idea of garlanding columns and water jars. Roses, acanthus, carnations, hyacinths, double anemones, staff flowers, and oak, laurel, bay, and acanthus leaves were used for this purpose.

The early Romans on the whole scorned to practice the arts themselves. They felt art beneath them and left such things as floral arrangement to their slaves. Yet, as the Latin poets prove, even the Roman patrician had a keen appreciation of hue and value, form, and exquisite detail in flower and fruit. During the decline of the Roman Empire, flowers (mainly roses) were used profusely to decorate banquet tables and bathing pavilions. These were grown out of season among the pipes used to heat the public baths. Roses were imported from Egypt and other countries around the Mediterranean. The flowers were not arranged but were strewn carelessly on tables, couches, and in the streets, where they were trampled by the victorious legions returning from conquest. There seemed to be as little regard for the preservation of plant material as for the Christian martyrs thrown to the lions.

Medieval Europe

During this period, flower arranging was carried on mostly by the monks who tended walled gardens adjacent to their monasteries. They made arrangements chiefly for their Romanesque and Gothic churches. Lilies, carnations, columbine, morning-glory, roses, hearts-ease (viola), bleeding heart, and violets were used. As shown in paintings of that era, they were placed in narrow-necked vases. With few flowers the monks expressed aspiration and pious thought by using formal, elongated vertical lines. Our own one-flower compositions are reminiscent of some medieval floral arrangements.

The Renaissance

During this era, the fall of Constantinople in 1453 caused great change in the world of art. People came closer to the beauty in nature. Floral decoration flourished. Floral compositions depicted in tapestries woven by noblewomen of the period for adornment of walls in churches and manor houses offer evidence of this. The various arts were patronized by rich noblemen. The great Chaucer's verse is filled with references to garden flowers. Like the Greeks, the people of the Renaissance used floral material for personal adornment and for garlanding rather than in containers; however, both tapestries and stained-glass windows in the cathedrals of Europe show arrangements of flowers and fruit. Religious paintings and poetry indicate that certain flowers had symbolic significance. (See Appendix II, Symbolism of Plant Materials.)

Baroque Period

During the late Renaissance, the Italians became famous for their beautiful gardens, in which herbs and such flowers as lilies and roses were cultivated. Their formal, massive, and ornate arrangements reflected their manner of living. Often an accessory—a stuffed bird or animal—was used with an arrangement for a home; but arrangements for churches were composed with restraint. Fruits were also combined with flowers. A certain form of vase which permitted only the heads of flowers to show became very popular. Arrangements during this period were rich in color and curvilinear in design.

Later, styles in furnishings and architecture became lighter in feeling, even frivolous. In France, much rococo ornamentation and curved design were used. Flowers were much in evidence and were used abundantly to decorate cathedrals, large halls, and reception rooms.

Dutch and Flemish

During the 17th century in Europe a new world trade grew up. Many flowers and seeds were imported into Flanders and Holland from Africa, China, and the Americas. Flemish artists painted flowers not previously seen in Europe. As a result, a great impetus was given to floral art. Church decorations were simple and symbolic; while secular ones were more opulent. A great variety of deep-colored flowers harmonized with richly carved furniture and elaborately ornamented vases. The flowers most often seen were roses, delphiniums, larkspur, African marigolds, nasturtiums, giant sunflowers, tulips. The reverse side of leaves was often turned to give rhythmic effect, and petals on tulips were reflexed to add interest.

American Colonies

The colonists who set out for the New World brought a few of their precious furnishings from their native lands; but church decorations were scarce. The cherished pewter jugs and earthenware bowls of New England were used to hold arrangements of field flowers and herbs. The wealthier colonists of the post-Revolutionary era imported handsome furnishings in the heavy style of the late Renaissance. They also imported plants. These made themselves at home on New World soil. Together with the rich, colorful native plants of the Americas, they provided abundant material for massed floral arrangements after the Flemish style, as well as for the simple but beautiful mixed bouquets suitable for meetinghouses and the plain living and high thinking of New England. Rosemary, sweet William, tansy, trumpet vine, verbena, wallflower, pink, columbine, hyacinth, lily, marigold, mint, narcissus, phlox, cornflower, honesty, cattail, primrose, rose, tulip, violet, artimesia, aster, black-eyed Susan, fruit blossom, monkshood, peony, petunia, poppy, and moss roses were brought in from gardens or culled from the fields to adorn churches, mantelpieces, and the oak, pine, or fruit-wood tables of the colonists.

18th-Century France

In France at the time of Louis XIV, floral arrangements were on a grand scale. Sumptuousness of living was evident. Rich velvety roses, pansies, and other flowers were used to harmonize with the velvets and satins of the elegant clothes of the aristocracy. Flowers of delicate hue were also used in arrangements for churches and were keyed to the newer light colors of wall hangings, also to the delicacy of church architecture. Delphinium, poppy, larkspur, columbine, and anemone are shown in paintings, combined with roses, acacia, begonias, carnations, camellias, iris, lilac, and peony. Other flowers rich in color and texture were arranged in curvilinear design. These were beauti-

FIG. 6. This study of delicate, lovely spring flowers is appropriate for a wedding. Soft pink herbaceous peonies and lavender wisteria make the arrangement look as airy as the breeze. The pastel colors are related to the French style in the glass container.

ful against the mauve, French blue, and gray backgrounds of the day. Churches and cathedrals were decorated with simplicity.

Georgian England

Great interest was shown in cultivating new varieties of plants brought back by scouts from the New World. It became fashionable among the clerics to grow sweet-scented herbs in church gardens. Urn-shaped vases of Grecian influence were used to complement the delicate window traceries in cathedrals and homes filled with classic furniture turned out by Sheraton, Hepplewhite, and Chippendale. Toward the close of the 17th century, interest in the ruins of Pompeii influenced a change in the types of vases used. The Grecian amphora (two-handled vase) became popular and was copied by ceramic factories. Trade with China and Japan also brought beautiful containers to Britain's shores. Gold and Sheffield plate were used extensively for altar containers. The flowers used in them were lilacs, roses, carnations, dahlias, day lilies, delphiniums, Easter lilies, foxglove, gladiolus, iris, larkspur, lupin, daisies, marigolds, pansies, peonies, petunias, and tulips.

The United States

In the newly formed United States, many containers of glass, salt glaze, silver, pottery, and pewter began to be imported from Europe. Equally cherished were the fine porcelains from China and Japan. American craftsmen developed skill and grace in their designs of furniture made from Caribbean mahogany; native pine and fruit wood were seen in the furnishings of churches. To harmonize with these, the arts of silversmith and glassmaker were called into being. By the end of the Revolution, the former colonists had developed a style and taste of their own. Their churches were adorned with mass arrangements of flowers and fruits, unsophisticated, simple, and appropriate to life in a new democracy.

19th Century

This century ushered in the Regency period in England, the Empire in France, and the Federalist in America. It was a period of commercial expansion. The French Revolution had given the middle classes control in that country. Under Napoleon, the period acquired a military flavor. Life tended to become simpler and more academic. Neoclassicism emerged in the arts, and solid rectilinear design supplanted the curvilinear in furnishings. Flower arrangements were stiff and followed, to a degree, geometric forms. Flowers were not used as profusely as later on, in the Victorian period. However, aster, bleeding heart, Canterbury bell, chrysanthemum, cornflower, forget-me-not, fruit blossom, fuchsia, holly, hyacinth, iris, larkspur, pansy, poppy, petunia, peony, rose, ranunculus, snapdragon, stock, sweet William, and tulip were among those used.

Victorian Period

During the long reign of Queen Victoria of England, mass arrangement of flowers reached its height, becoming as overstuffed in style as was the upholstered furniture of the day. Seedpods and

Photo Russell Illig   *Fern Bowers Hunt*

FIG. 7. Snapdragons and carnations are built up in conical form to repeat the cone shape of the milk glass container. The flowers are surrounded at the base by green-veined, white caladium leaves. This vertical arrangement would be suitable for an Early American church where the woodwork is painted white.

grasses were combined lavishly with brilliantly colored blooms; flowers under glass were seen everywhere. Containers were ornate and of designs which today seem overdecorated for floral art. They were made of Bohemian glass, lusterware, ironstone, Belleek, and Haviland china. But floral decorations for churches tended to show more restraint than those in homes. Anemone, bleeding heart, bluebell, carnation, clover, cockscomb, cornflower, coreopsis, dahlia, daisy, forget-me-not, foxglove, fuchsia, geranium, godetia, heather, hyacinth, jasmine, lilac, magnolia, tulip, and mignonette were used.

The Orient

Four centuries had gone by since the adventurous spirits of the Western world opened water routes between the Eastern and Western Hemispheres. Goods and ideas had been freely shared. Flowers and plants from the East had changed the European and American landscapes. Objects of art from India, China, Japan, and the islands of the East Indies had been brought as treasure-trove to European and American households. But the art of arranging plant material, the purely Oriental expression of the relationship of Nature and Man through floral arrangement, was not grasped until the present century. This fascinating art, with its simple rules of design, came to Japan from India by way of China and Korea. It came to America mainly through Japan.

It is recorded that flower arrangement first took place in India. After heavy storms, Buddhist priests, who frowned on waste in plant and animal life, would salvage blossoms blown down by the winds. These they placed in water. Pleased with the effect, they continued the practice of arranging plant material. This theory of the earliest beginning of floral decoration is reasonable enough to have led one author after another to borrow the idea and pass it on. The art spread with Buddhism to China, and to it the Chinese added their concept of beauty by constructing mass arrangements of flowers.

China was known as the Flowery Kingdom and the Mother of Gardens because early artists in their works led the world to believe China to be full of flowers. An ancient Chinese poet wrote:

> The East wind is blowing
> The grass of Yung-Chow is green
> The voice of spring is heard all over
> By a thousand gateways, by ten thousand doorways.

Photo Russell Illig   *Fern Bowers Hunt*

FIG. 8. Mass arrangement of late summer flowers in autumnal shades are placed in a copper container. This type of composition would be suitable for a mantel or a chest. It shows a Chinese influence.

Another wrote:

> *If you keep a green bough in your heart,*
> *The singing bird will come.*

Later, when Buddhism had spread to Japan, the idea of using plant material for artistic purposes fell on fertile soil. The Japanese people, with their innate love of beauty and natural materials, took the art of flower arrangement to their hearts and made it their own.

In the 15th century, the Regent Prince of Japan, Yoshimasa, Eighth Ashikaga Shogun, became a patron of the arts and inaugurated the Tea Ceremony (a religious practice). He appointed professors of the ceremony to encourage both rich and poor to study the art of flower arrangement. They simplified mass arrangements into

Photo Russell Illig   *Fern Bowers Hunt*

FIG. 9. This line arrangement shows a strong Oriental influence. Graceful sprays of pink Japanese plum are placed in a pewter copper-washed container. This type of arrangement is suitable for mantel or chest in a small recreation room of a church.

graceful linear ones and wove their love of nature into their compositions. To them, flower arrangement was inspirational, for they believed that a religious spirit, self-denial, and gentleness were virtues to be practiced in this art. Because of stimulated interest in flower arrangement, many schools of the art came into being throughout Japan. So intent were the people regarding it that different schools of thought sprang up. One of these taught the theory of a tri-element arrangement symbolizing Heaven, Man, and Earth. This idea was conceived by Soami, a celebrated painter and friend of Yoshimasa. The following outline gives its principles:

1. **Heaven (or Shin).** Topmost and strongest branch. It may be bent to bow out in a graceful curve but must return until directly above place where stem rests on pin holder in formal style.

2. **Man (or Soya).** Secondary branch, weaker than Heaven line and two thirds its length, is brought forward from the base to form one side of a triangle when viewed from above.

3. **Earth (or Tai).** The third or tertiary line is cut one third the length of the Man line. It is placed on the other side of the Heaven line and tipped forward, thus completing a triangle when viewed from above or when facing it. The tip ends of Man and Earth lines always face toward the Heaven branch.

Other branches that conform with Man and Earth lines in contour may be inserted between Man and Heaven, and between Earth and Heaven, but never placed outside this boundary.

Another Japanese school of thought instituted five-element arrangements using (1) earth; (2) fire; (3) water; (4) metal; (5) wood.

A third group symbolized the virtues of the human heart to denote lines of arrangement.

The Japanese also applied sex distinctions to plant material. A branch strong and angular, or a flower bold in color, symbolized man, while the delicate, weaker branches or flowers, rounded in form, denoted woman.

The Japanese practiced bending and shaping leaves and branches so that the beautiful reverse side might be used. Bending and shaping is accomplished by placing stems in deep water for four hours or more; when pliable they may be gently twisted and bent over the left thumb.

In developing the art of flower arrangement, the Japanese teachers suggested certain principles of composition that are used extensively today:

1. Choose graceful branches in different stages of growth: buds, half-blown flowers, those fully blossomed out.

2. Cut branches 1½ to 5 times or more the height or width of the container, for a line arrangement.

3. Plant material in an arrangement must appear to be growing naturally. This is accomplished by keeping the stems of branches and flowers close together for about 4 inches above the point where they emerge from the holder.

4. Flowers and plant material must be fresh and free from disease.

5. Branches should not cross in an arrangement.

6. No two branches of equal length should be placed side by side.

7. No "window-cutting" where stem lines cross and recross and form loops.

8. No double streamers, where branches droop on both sides. Drooping lines allowed only on one side of an arrangement.

9. No "dew-spilling" where blossoms and leaves touch table top.

10. No "nail-heading" where flat-headed blossoms are stepped up in orderly sequence.

11. No "color-sandwiching" where a bloom of one color is placed between two of another color or strong contrast in value.

12. No lines pointing directly forward or back (guest-pokers or wall-pokers).

13. No lines of equal length. The Japanese believe variety is obtained by asymmetrical balance which is more interesting than symmetrical.

14. Flowers and foliage should not touch the container's sides.

15. Trim overlapping foliage so that flowers may show to advantage.

16. Maintain rhythmic feeling in plant material by repeating colors, lines, and forms.

17. Use only uneven numbers of leaves and blossoms in an arrangement.

The Japanese style in arrangements follows nature. The arranger should strive to forget his usual cares and express his feelings through natural materials. His arrangements should offer more than decoration—they should offer inspiration to both the arranger and the observer.

East Meets West in 20th-Century America

The 20th century opened an age of mechanical invention overlaid with much sentimental romanticism. Many styles in furnishings and architecture were revived—the neoclassic of the 1880's, the Flemish style of the 1700's, the Spanish mission style drifting eastward from California—even a pseudo-return to the style of the Middle Ages in the use of stained-glass windows and arched niches and heavy draperies. Flowers such as roses, delphiniums, peonies, tulips, forget-me-nots, and lilies were used in stiff and opulent arrangements in urn-shaped containers. The medieval influence also brought single-flower compositions in vases of silver into popularity. The first years of the century were years of flaunted wealth in flower arrangements as in other arts. But out of all this confusion and imitation of past epochs of glory grew signs of growth, of searching for means of self-expression and of ways to use the new ideas, new materials that had become available.

A new school of architecture was rising, mainly in Germany, France, Scandinavia, and the United States. The influences that inspired its

Photo Russell Illig   *Fern Bowers Hunt*

Fig. 10. Line-mass arrangement was composed of a Watsonia stalk and yellow and green pandanus to give it height. Combined with these are yellow roses in various stages of bloom, and leaves of the peperomia plant. This composition is suitable for a narrow panel in an entry. It is contemporary in style.

originators were from the old civilizations of Asia, Africa, and South America. Many of the materials with which they built and the uses to which their structures were put were new to the world. Functional contemporary design was first put to use in factories, railway stations, and skyscrapers—places hardly lending themselves to new concepts of floral arrangement. Only much later was the philosophy of the modern architect applied to churches and homes for middle-class Americans. With emphasis on open space in these contemporary churches and frequent use of structural glass to make the transition from the interior to the out of doors came a sudden understanding of and sympathy with the simple, dramatic flower arrangements of the Orient.

During the past twenty years the whole art of floral decoration has been revolutionized. The formal mass concepts of the Chinese have been adapted to our less ornate contemporary church buildings. Line arrangements, borrowed directly from the Japanese, are seldom placed on an altar but are used in parish house and social rooms. The principles of good design can be applied with equal skill when the setting and plant material dictate a traditional mass arrangement derived from the European style. For example, contemporary arrangements are simple and uncluttered, often employing broad leaves and flowers simple in form. These are usually placed in open-mouthed containers chosen for shape, color, and texture rather than for ostentation. There is, however, growing up in America and elsewhere a new thought in floral design, one that disregards the nature of plant material and encourages its distortion in arrangements.

A number of reasons for this come to mind: floral art has not kept pace with architecture, sculpture, and other three-dimensional art forms. Education has lagged in this field, in spite of the fact that teachers of garden-club courses, many junior colleges, and adult school classes are bending every effort to keep it free of artificiality and distortion. However, when an art mushrooms as this one has, there is always danger of decadence. People are inclined to forget the tenets on which an art is based, especially when there is mass production to serve it. During approximately the past fifteen years, manufacturers have been busy bringing to a ready market many articles for arrangements such as containers, figurines, all sorts of mechanical aids, and kindred accessories. Some are of good design, some deplorably bad. Growers, too, have been busy supplying the demand for unusual plant material. Unfortunately, much of this material is being dyed, painted, flocked, and otherwise distorted by people of undeveloped taste, so that any likeness to its naturally beautiful state, either living or dried, is purely coincidental. An arranger should be as honest as a good architect is with his building materials. Brick is not made to look like marble or vice versa, nor does one see false shutters, false pillars or façades on a well-designed building.

It is generally agreed among artists that if an art is to endure, it must show refinement in craft and taste. The materials must be used in a manner consistent with their nature and for the purpose intended. If we are to raise standards in this field, we must free our minds from the erroneous idea that floral design should be patterned after abstract modern painting. The two art forms differ widely as to materials, dimensions, techniques, and terminology. And yet many arrangers are using books on painting to guide them in their design and terminology.

Painting is a point, line, figure, and flat plane art having two dimensions, either length or height, and breadth, known as area. A painter wishing to give a feeling of the third dimension must employ tone, shadow, and perspective. The materials he uses are inanimate. He knows he can only approximate a representation of a being or a flower; he does not often try, preferring to render his design in the abstract, a distortion of natural objects. Conversely, the arranger works with spatial design; his materials are living (or, if dried, once were) all are three-dimensional, having height, width, and thickness.

To apply the terminology of solid geometry in our concepts of design in mass arrangements, we build a *spherical* arrangement, not a circular one; an *ellipsoid*, not an ellipse; a *pyramid*, not a triangle.

Good taste and the law of inseparable association demand that the components of a good floral composition be arranged according to their distinguishing quality, in agreement with their habit of growth. For example, fuchsias and grapes grow pendulously and should be so arranged; delphinium and calla lilies grow tall and upright and look best when placed upright. Nature provides long, graceful stems to support their heavy heads. To arrange these flowers in low bowls with their heads chopped off from their stems is to lose half their beauty, since we subconsciously associate natural materials with the way we have seen them growing and are disturbed when they are arranged in a contrary position. Christ said, "Consider the lilies . . . how they grow."

Christmas, First Methodist Church, Palo Alto, Calif.

Grace Cathedral, San Francisco, Calif.

3

The Creativity of Floral Art

If of thy mortal goods thou art bereft
And from thy slender store two loaves alone to thee are left;
Sell one, and with the dole
Buy hyacinths to feed thy soul.

So said Sadi, the great Persian poet of the 13th century, and his words ring true and meaningful today. Perhaps the real significance of floral decoration for the church lies in a people's deep longing and need for the beauty in nature. To satisfy this need, now as in ancient days, cut flowers are brought indoors and arranged in water to keep them for a time so that their form, color, and texture may be viewed at closer range and their fragrances and pungent odors enjoyed. This primal need may account for the widespread and growing interest in the art of floral arrangement for churches. The noted connoisseur, Bernard Berenson, states beautifully this universal response to natural beauty: "As I walk in the garden, I look at the flowers and shrubs and trees and discover in them an exquisiteness of contour, a vitality of edge, an infinite variety of color that no artifact I have seen can rival." While he does not mention fragrance, I am sure one so perceptive would not overlook so charming an attribute.

An arrangement of beautiful flowers or branches is a direct way of expressing one's feeling of reverence in a holy place. Growing things speak a universal language. Through them we can make known our joy in Christ's birth and in His Resurrection, in the arrival and blessing of the newborn, felicitations for the newly wed, celebration of an anniversary, condolence in illness and sorrow, and comfort in bereavement. Floral decoration is of the very substance of celebration of the Church's great festivals as well as its weekly services. A floral arrangement may be used to lead attention to the cross on the altar, as a focal point of emphasis in a sanctuary, and at the same time link symbolically to the vestment of a special day.

The communication we derive from floral art is one of naturalness and intrinsic beauty. For the arranger, these values are to be obtained:

1. By communicating the arranger's ideas, a composition may please and satisfy the senses of sight, smell, and touch.

2. It may offer a therapeutic, creative interest to the arranger; it may also lift the spirit of a viewer possibly ill or disturbed.

3. Knowledge of the art develops an appreciation of good design and may encourage other kindred interests.

4. Acquaintance with the wide variety of plant material available and suitable for arrangement deepens one's knowledge of plant life and habits of growth.

5. A common interest in and pursuit of the art can be shared by a group of people, and ideas exchanged.

6. Through teaching, children can be encouraged in conservation by suggestions for growing their own plants for arranging, rather than borrowing too greedily from nature's storehouse.

So conceived, floral arrangement takes its rightful place as one of the visual arts.

In all forms of art, the medium with which an artist works must be adaptable and appropriate to its purpose and concordant with its nature. Beauty does not affect everyone in the same way. What is beautiful to one individual may not always please another. Each will view an arrangement and enjoy it in the light of his own knowledge. Beauty has been charmingly explained by Walter Crane in his book on line and form: "Beauty is so delicate a quality, so complex in its elements, a question often of such nice balance and judgment— depending upon a hair's breadth difference in the poise of a mass here, or the sweep of a curve there—that we cannot weave technical nets fine enough to catch so sensitive a butterfly. She is indeed a Psyche in art, both seeking and sought, to be won only by devotion and love."

To be beautiful, a floral arrangement must have certain fundamental qualities present in its make-up. Like every work of art, it must have unity, variety, and emphasis. These in turn encompass selectivity, distinction, appropriateness, simplicity, harmony, and expression.

Unity is achieved by careful selection of plant material, container, and kindred accessories which are alike in an associative way. There must be agreement between parts of the whole, such as in forms and lines, and a careful and harmonious blending of colors, sizes, and textures. The arrangement must be right in feeling for the occasion, appropriate to its setting, to the time of day and season of year. As an example, a unified and appropriate decoration for a Romanesque or Byzantine church at Christmas would be Della Robbia wreaths and garlands designed to follow the semicircular arched openings of either style. These should be skillfully made of laurel or other strong-bodied, broad leaves. Superimposed in a pleasing design should be such symbolic fruits as pomegranates, lemons, apples, grapes, and oranges. If the music were Gregorian and if the service followed the Nativity story, one could say the decorations were in unity with church and service.

Variety in size, texture, spaces, color, length of line, and form adds interest to any composition. The transition from one to another of these should be gradual. This may be accomplished by using buds and filler material, also by gradation in size of flowers or fruits.

Emphasis is achieved by introduction into the arrangement of a dominant feature, the purpose of which is to hold attention within the framework of the composition, and not at its outer limits. It is important that there be but one focal point, otherwise attention is distracted. The emphatic point, for example, could be an open-faced flower emerging from a structure of buds or smaller flowers; or a flower of striking color surrounded by contrasting or gradating colors in flowers. The dominant feature may be brought into focus by transitional plant material. The point of emphasis is placed where axes cross or lines converge in the arrangement. If for any reason the emphatic point seems too dominant, it may be softened with delicate, airy plant material placed around it. If it seems too weak, then contrasting colors or values in leaves may be grouped around the dominant features to dramatize it. The focal point of interest must never become so important as to detract attention from the whole. A plane passing through its location may determine one's frame of reference.

If plant material has sufficient emphasis in itself to lead the attention *into* the arrangement, it isn't always necessary to place a dominant flower or object at a spot where lines converge and axes cross. In illustration, flowering branches placed in a container will carry the eye of the observer down each stem to the point whereon they impinge on the flower-holder. If balance is present and the holder is concealed, such an arrangement would be successful.

Selectivity is an invaluable determinant in the total effect of an arrangement. The perceptive worker strives to find plant material that is completely fresh, crisp, and free from blemish. It must be appropriate to his preconceived purpose and plan. The search for unusual lines and forms, and also subtle colors, to suit a particular container or an important background space, is a rewarding one, for the effort often results in elevating an arrangement above the commonplace, provided it is skillfully composed, and shows a certain amount of originality.

Distinction is the expression of an arranger's idea. It is characteristic of his individuality and personality. It cannot be imposed by others nor can it be wholly defined. Perhaps the preceding paragraph comes fairly close, for selectivity and distinction are closely linked. To be completely original, the plant material, container, and design must be new to the arranger. This is not always possible, of course, because in many places an arranger has only a limited amount of plant material to choose from and must use the containers provided by the church. But triteness can be avoided by handling material in skillful ways to achieve a distinctive arrangement, always adhering to basic principles of design.

The aspect of originality should not cause too great concern, for a congregation does not look for something different each week in floral containers, any more than it expects something different in the music. If the music is of the highest order possible and if the flowers are beautiful and well arranged, their purpose is accomplished.

Appropriateness in an arrangement denotes its suitability for the occasion, time, place, and the particular church for which it is planned. A charming arrangement of calendulas for a church breakfast would hardly be appropriate at a formal Easter service; an arrangement composed mainly of orchids for a wedding reception would be sadly out of place at a barbecue.

Simplicity and restraint are prime considerations in both church and secular floral decoration. One should not contrive ludicrous arrangements, slavishly follow fads, or attempt to attract the observer with pretentious or bizarre effects. The all-embracing purpose of a floral arrangement in any part of the church is to show flowers to the best possible advantage and to suit them to the service or the occasion and to the place they are to occupy. Simplicity is the absence of extraneous plant material and distracting decoration in the design of an arrangement or its container. The trend in contemporary church and home decoration is toward simple uncluttered lines and forms, since these are restful and satisfying. Simplicity connotes sincerity—honesty in the treatment of plant materials. It is a quality much to be desired and is always a hallmark of good taste.

Harmony is the element of consistency that makes a composition aesthetically pleasing. There should be orderly arrangement of shapes, sizes, textures, and colors, and a feeling of concord should pervade

Photo William Arborgast   *Roberta Pleas*

FIG. 11. *Woodside Village Church, Woodside, Calif.* Winter stock, marguerites, and mock orange are used for this altar arrangement for Holy Saturday, when the Paschal candle is lighted.

Photo Russell Illig   *Fern Bowers Hunt*

FIG. 12. A line arrangement of pink flowering plum shows a strong Oriental influence. These blossoms were cut in the early bud stage, placed in deep water near light in a warm room. In this way the color in each flower is much more delicate than when allowed to come into bloom in the garden.

the whole. Spherical arrangements look best on round tabletops; rectangular arrangements against rectangular backgrounds—providing there is adequate space around the arrangement; small flowers in small vases; rough-textured plants, such as succulents, with pottery or wood; velvety flowers with fine-textured glazes, silver or glass, and sympathetic blending of colors all make for harmony. Delicate Venetian glass vases filled with violets would hardly strike a harmonious note in a parish room where the men's club was scheduled to meet, but they might set the tone of decoration for a gathering of the women's auxiliary. Nor does one place coarse-fleshed cacti in a silver bowl which better should contain roses.

Expression is that quality in an arrangement that suggests a mood or tells a story. A good arrangement *does* something; it presents an idea (see page 40). Expression is a quality of aliveness that gives charm to a composition which otherwise would seem static or dull. In flower arrangement, I think of this as being akin to exaltation, so called to describe the impetus to live, present in all plants. Although cut from the parent stalk, flowers turn their faces or tip ends toward the light. In plant culture, this is known as heliotropism. To employ this element of time—in actuality as well as in feeling—the plant is cut before it comes to full bloom, and as the buds open they assume interesting shapes and delightful positions. Plants like snapdragon, gladiolus, lupin, bells of Ireland, tritoma, when arranged in bud form, turn their tip ends up like candles. Calendula, tithonia, nasturtium, and others rearrange themselves in a container and take on lines more

Photo Russell Illig   *Fern Bowers Hunt*

FIG. 13. This composition of red roses in a pewter bowl is appropriate for any day that honors a martyred saint. It would also be appropriate at any time for a desk or table decoration in an office of the church or its recreation rooms.

Photo Russell Illig   *Fern Bowers Hunt*

FIG. 14. Arrangement of geraniums with three birds as the focal point is an interesting type of arrangement to teach children size relationship in floral design and also an excellent way to teach them how to tell a story by using figurines.

graceful than we can hope to approach by calculated effort. The branches of flowering trees and shrubs, when cut in bud stage and placed in water, will come into bloom if given light (but not direct sunlight), surprising us with their grace and charm. They will be free of sunburn and windburn and insect infestation, and, of course, are more delicate in color and much longer lasting than those left to bloom in the garden.

Expressiveness can be created by suggested movement. The writer can think of no more telling analogy than a fine wood carving, say, of an eagle in flight, or one of a marathon runner bent to the wind. This same feeling may be achieved in floral arrangement by employing strong primary lines that are rhythmic, using branches whose tip ends diminish, as in slender tips of foliage or in slim buds, or by progression of size in flowers. If these lines are placed at the outer perimeter of an arrangement, a feeling of movement results. Gradations of color from dark to light (in value) suggest movement, as do blossoms all facing in one direction. With this dynamic feeling in an arrangement, the imagination may have full sway. It may be approximated with a figurine in the wind-blown effect so often seen in fine ceramics, and arrangements using figurines in interesting stances can be made a way of teaching children Biblical stories.

4

Elements of Design in Floral Art

Floral art may be defined as spatial design in which growing plant material is the medium of creative expression. With inherent good taste, people in many countries and in every era have engaged in the practice of floral decoration, and, through trial and error, a number of craftsmen have brought it to a high degree of development. Since some people are more perceptive than others in this field, and since the rudimentary principles underlying good design are based on nature's laws, it follows that the observant ones are those who have benefited most from this art.

In flower arranging, the basic elements used are line, form, and shape found in plant material and kindred accessories, together with their attributes of texture, color, and often fragrance. Using these, the arranger can create interesting space divisions in the way materials are placed, and can evolve beautiful patterns (silhouettes) with them.

Line. Certain linear materials found in the plant world are designated for line arrangements, such as the slender whiplike branches of trees, shrubs, and vines. Lines are placed in an arrangement to provide the scaffold or structure. Basic lines may be straight, angular, or curvilinear, or variations and combinations of these. Lines express movement, force, show direction. Straight lines are "fast" lines, meandering or curved lines, "slow." Line material (meaning stems) sometimes is thought of as having only two dimensions; it really has three: length, width, and thickness. You can pick up a stem and look at it from every side. (See line arrangements on page 38.)

Fig. 15. Vertical arrangement of narcissi in open-mouthed container. This is a simple
but effective study. It would be pleasing on a desk, a small table, or on a mantel.

Form is an important element of design in floral decoration. Like
architecture, sculpture, and ceramics, it is three-dimensional. The five
basic geometrical forms found in plant materials and including fruit,
containers, and accessories, are sphere, cylinder, prism, cone, and
pyramid, and variations and combinations of these. All these objects
have concrete form. For example, a double rose is spherical, a single
one disc-shaped; delphinium spikes are conical; and an orange, apple,

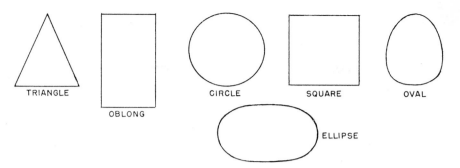

TWO-DIMENSIONAL FIGURES OF AREA USED IN DRAWING
AND PAINTING

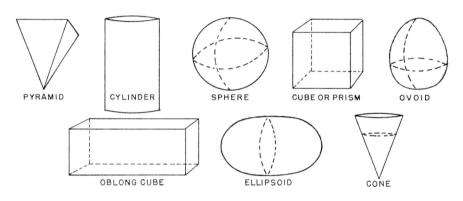

BASIC THREE-DIMENSIONAL FORMS KNOWN AS VOLUME
FOUND IN PLANT MATERIALS, CONTAINERS, AND FLORAL
ARRANGEMENTS

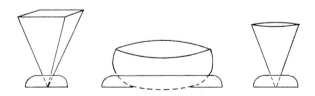

THE EYE WISHES TO SEE THE COMPLETED FORM WHERE
IT MEETS THE TABLE TOP, HENCE THE NEED FOR A BASE

Robert Miller

FIG. 16

43

FIG. 17. *First Congregational Church, Palo Alto, Calif.* White and purple grapes, together with apples, pomegranates, and grape leaves decorate the altar of this contemporary type church. A sheaf of cereal grain placed at the foot of the cross emphasizes this Thanksgiving holiday.

or plum is spherical, while a watermelon or cantaloupe is ellipsoidal. Any container is three-dimensional, else it could not hold water. Since it is always part and parcel of an arrangement, its height, width, and exterior thickness must be considered. On the inside, measuring downward from top to base, the dimension is referred to as depth. Volume is mass given shape which may be either thick or hollow.

Form in container and plant material should be chosen to suit each other and the planned background space. Spherical containers holding curvilinear plant material will look best against a background that repeats their contour, such as semicircular arches or niches; straightlined materials look best in straight-sided containers in front of vertical panels. Large and small forms used together should be unified by intermediate ones. Forms that are alike in an associative way connote the same general feeling and thus provide unity in the design. Pomegranates, grapefruit, oranges, grapes, apples all express bounteous plenty. The illustration on page 44 shows a simple, satisfying arrangement suitable for a church altar at Thanksgiving or Christmas.

The shape of leaves is three-dimensional because they are objects in space and have breadth, length, and a certain amount of thickness, depending on the type. Leaves may be round, palmate, trilobed, heart-shaped, arrow-shaped, ovate, etc.

Space divisions in an arrangement are as important as lines and forms. Spaces should be varied to avoid monotony and for balance. For instance, in placing an arrangement in a rectangular container, place the pin frog at a point a little more than one third the length of the long side and a little less than one half the short side to achieve pleasing space division. Never divide a surface in equal parts, as it offers no variety. Spacing between stems is also important—long stems close together, shorter ones farther apart. Variety in unity is an age-old axiom in art, and interesting space divisions make beautiful patterns.

Pattern is the silhouette of an arrangement against a background space. To be successful, the pattern must be interesting; lines and forms should present a pleasing outline. There must be variety in spacing, unevenness of lines, variety in forms, contrast in values and shapes, but never lines that cross and recross. There must be a feeling of equilibrium, good proportion; all objects used must be in proper scale. It has been said that to succeed with pattern in any contemporary building, we must show simplicity and strength of pattern. This may be accomplished in floral decoration by using bold, colorful flowers or leaves and striving for simplicity of design in the whole composition.

Texture is the surface quality presented by an arrangement—the roughness or smoothness of plant material, container, and accessories. Consistency in texture does not imply exact similarity; while texture may vary, it is important that vases, plant material, and general church or room furnishings be harmonious, for texture sets its own mood and style and should always be carefully considered. Rough textures are often duller than smooth textures; because of the presence of shadows, they absorb light. They are most suitable in the rustic type of church, on a terrace, or in a predominantly masculine church room. Smooth, satiny textures reflect light; thus, shiny flowers and vases are more appropriate in a more formal type of church or in rooms used especially by women.

Fragrance. *"For we are of the fragrance of Christ for God, alike as regards those who are saved and those who are lost."*

As has been stated so many times and in so many different ways, "All art speaks a universal language, and each medium with which an artist works speaks a particular one." Fragrance is a delightful component of many plants. Whenever possible, flowers with a pleasing scent should be used. (See list on page 188.)

Color is one of the most important elements in floral design. The attention of the beholder is attracted by color before he becomes aware of other factors entering into the design. In a church, color in a flower arrangement may be employed as a point of emphasis, to key to the vestments and other furnishings, such as altar hangings, and to tie the colors in the composition to those of plant material seen through a glass wall in a contemporary church. Extensive use of floor-to-ceiling glass and development of outdoor areas necessitate careful consideration of harmony of colors both without and within. Since color plays such an important part in the art of floral decoration, and because we are affected by it symbolically, emotionally, and aesthetically, it behooves the arranger to understand its many connotations and to learn to use them harmoniously.

No rigid directive or set formula can be offered to this desired end. There are numerous theories and systems, none of which has been standardized. Methods based primarily on the mixing of pigments are not suitable in floral arrangement. A widely different technique must be used by the arranger, for in this art the colors are not mixed

Photo Russell Illig

Fern Bowers Hunt

FIG. 18. Masses of lavender lilacs and pink primroses make a fragrant pyramidal arrangement suitable for the traditional type church.

but are placed side by side. To illustrate, a painter working with pigment and binder mixes violet and yellow (complementary colors) and produces a dull gray. Diametrically opposite is the arranger's process of placing these two colors side by side in a flower arrangement; here the result is strong contrast. The arranger's problem, then, is to combine effectively the colors in flowers and other plant material to achieve a harmonious, integrated whole.

Once the arranger accepts the challenge of the chameleon traits of colors in flowers and learns the proper use of them, truly beautiful chromatic compositions can be created. Keeping these factors in mind, it is likewise necessary to understand something of color terminology. In this chapter we shall use the pigment color theory, but we should also understand what is meant by spectrum colors.

Spectrum hues are those seen in a rainbow, through a spectroscope, or produced when a prism is held over a white surface and sunlight allowed to pass through it. Not all colors have hue. White, gray, and black are known as colors, or acromats. White is the combination of all colors reflected; black is the combination of all colors—it absorbs all color. Therefore, black and white are neutral and do not have hue. Gray is a combination of black and white, and it, too, is neutral and has no hue. Acromats, however, have value but no intensity.

Hue, then, is a term denoting different spectrum color names. Each will be known as a normal or standard color. Each hue has other properties such as value, intensity, luminosity, and texture.

Value or luminosity is the lightness or darkness of color, the degree of proximity to black or to white. When a color tends toward white and is lighter in value than its normal hue on the spectrum, it is known as a *tint*. As it tends toward darker than normal, it is known as a *shade*.

Intensity, chroma, saturation are the brightness or dullness of a normal hue. The intensity of a color can be dulled by adding or mixing it with its complement. Naturally, we do not mix pigments when we arrange flowers, but combine the colors that are present. If we wish dull hues, we must hunt for them. We may, however, seemingly tone down the intensity of bright flowers in an arrangement by adding gray foliage or white flowers. (Hues of like intensity form a key because of their relatedness.)

Texture. Arthur Guptill, in his book on color, admonishes the student of color to include texture, not as a quality such as intensity or value, but because the texture of any material affects its color. Hues are softened by rough textures because of the shadows present. Conversely, colors are heightened by shiny, smooth textures.

Light primaries are green, red, and violet-blue. When combined, they work up in value and are known as additive colors, because light added to light produces white, should these be converged from a projector on a white screen.

Pigment primaries are made up of chemicals, minerals, and animal matter. They are not pure color (as are light primaries). Pigment primaries are called subtractive colors because, when these are mixed, they work down in value and produce dull color or near black.

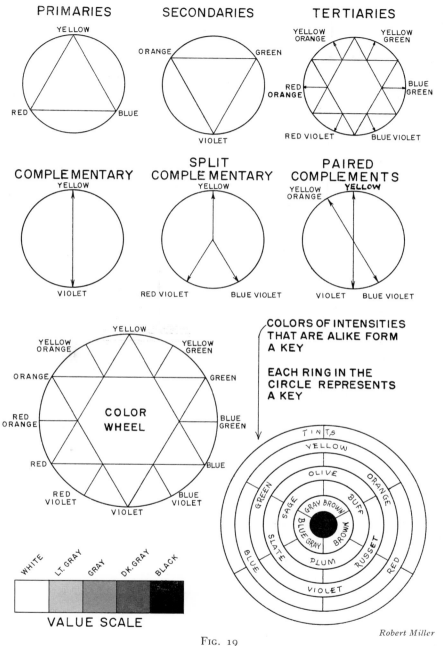

FIG. 19

Robert Miller

Primary Colors

Red   Yellow   Blue

These are the lowest common denominator of pigment color. From these three colors all pigment hues are evolved, but there is no color combination that will produce any of them. Many colorists suggest green-blue, red-violet, and yellow as pigment primaries. Because Garden Clubs, Incorporated, flower shows, and schools use red, yellow, and blue as their primary colors, I have adopted this simpler concept.

Secondary Colors

Orange is a combination of equal parts of red and yellow.
Green is a combination of equal parts of yellow and blue.
Violet is a combination of equal parts of blue and red.
Primary and secondary colors used together are called normal or standard primaries.

Tertiary Colors

Yellow-green is a combination of equal parts of yellow and green.
Blue-green is a combination of equal parts of blue and green.
Blue-violet is a combination of equal parts of blue and violet.
Red-violet is a combination of equal parts of red and violet.
Red-orange is a combination of equal parts of red and orange.
Yellow-orange is a combination of equal parts of yellow and orange.

It will help to standardize the names of colors if they are named as listed here and if the primary color in each admixture is named first, for example, blue-green or blue-blue-green. Often such fanciful names as peacock blue, air force blue, Mamie pink, coronation red, are given loosely to colors. This practice as applied to floral arrangement should be discouraged so that we may clarify and simplify the nomenclature of color.

You may have heard it said that in nature all colors seem to blend harmoniously. This is often true as it applies to blooms growing together in a field, for nature provides an expanse of sky, field, and distance and the play of sunlight and shadow to modify their hues. However, this largeness of setting is lost when plants of a variety of colors are brought indoors and placed in an arrangement to be viewed at closer range. The same colors that did not seem to clash outside may be disturbingly inharmonious in the intimacy of an arrangement.

The person wishing to advance in the art of floral composition, or one wishing to train for color judging, should understand and explore theories and systems of color. The light theory is practicable (at present) only for those working with colored lighting in the theater or in window displays. It should not concern the arranger except in the presentation of flower shows or when special lighting is called for in conjunction with floral decoration.

It *is* important that the blending of pigments be understood. I strongly advise anyone wishing to advance beyond the stage of rank beginner to make a color wheel. There is no better way of acquainting oneself with the basic principles of the pigment systems and the way that colors in flowers and background affect each other. Instructions for making a simple color wheel may be found on page 199.

Choosing Colors. In planning an arrangement, choose colors in plant materials that have an associative connotation with the idea you are trying to present, and keep appropriateness in mind. Light pink and blue flowers would not be thought of as ideal to arrange for a men's church dinner; black or orange flowers would never be used at an Easter service. Colors set a mood, even as textures do. Study each plant you choose for an arrangement. You may discover subtle combinations previously unobserved. In working with fruit, see how beautiful the persimmon, grape, and apple are when they change from yellow-green to orange, then to red. The intermediate or grayed colors of like intensity are the most subtle. Hues of this kind can lift an arrangement above the commonplace to a level of genuine interest and beauty.

Reflected colors act as harmonizers; they add depth and atmosphere. Satiny, shining surfaces reflect more color than rough ones. A mirror or colored metallic paper placed under a container of flowers on a table will harmonize a silver, pewter, or glass bowl with the colors in the flowers. Warm or yellowed lights reflect cool shadows, while cool violet-colored lights reflect warm shadows. Plan cool colors alone and warm ones alone in an arrangement; or one color dominant over the other. Avoid spotty effects by grading colors from light to dark and by using hues that lie close together on the color wheel. You will thus avoid holes in an arrangement that is to be reviewed from a distance.

The primary colors may be used together for dramatic effect, but an arrangement having them should be small, as these colors are unrelated and are too strident in a large arrangement. The illustration on page 2 is a good example of the dramatic use of primary colors.

The secondary colors are more pleasing than the primaries when used together because of their relatedness to each other. However, the intermediate colors lying equidistant from each other on the color wheel are even more pleasing than the secondaries, when used together. One should also choose colors in flowers that are alike in value; for instance, pastel colors of like value form a key.

Color Harmony

Monochromatic is a one-color scheme and is the easiest for a beginning arranger to follow. To illustrate, use one hue, such as red, and with it use only a lighter or darker hue such as pink, light pink, or dark red. These colors are related and are restful when used together. To avoid monotony in this type of scheme, vary values and the forms and sizes of flowers, and place the arrangement against a contrasting background. In this way you will achieve a pleasing and harmonious composition.

Analogous harmony is more interesting than the monochromatic, since it allows for greater latitude in choice of color. When working with this type, it is well to stay within the framework of a primary or color family. A color family contains only the steps from one primary to the next. For instance, select red as the dominant color; red, red-orange, and orange comprise the red family because each color has the hue red in its admixture. The next step brings you to yellow, which is the next primary. This you do not include. To avoid dullness, vary values and intensities or choose gray foliage. Analogous colors in flowers used together tend to be the most satisfying of all color combinations, because close intervals of color are always restful and rhythmic in feeling, provided they are used in orderly sequence.

Complementary or contrasting colors lie opposite each other on the color wheel. One sure way to find the complement of a hue is to stare at a color for a full minute. Slip a white card in front of the color stared at, and an afterimage will form and show the true complement. Stare at yellow and see violet. Stare at blue-green and see red. Paradoxically, you are seeing all color, because the complement is always an admixture of the two colors needed to complete a color circle. In flower arrangement, complementaries should be used with discretion—one in greater quantity than the other. Values should be varied, unless you wish strong contrast or a startling effect, because there is a wide interval between complementary colors. They are dramatic when placed side by side, but when mixed they produce gray. For church arrangements, whenever possible contrast the arrangement against a complementary background.

Split-complementary colors are those two colors lying at either side of a color's complement. The split complement of yellow will be blue-violet and red-violet, leaving out violet.

Paired complements are the two colors lying side by side and their complements. For instance, a harmony consisting of yellow and yellow-green plus violet and red-violet would be pleasing.

Triadic colors are three hues lying equidistant from one another on the color wheel. These are red, blue, yellow, and combinations of these colors that are also equidistant. Triadic colors are satisfying when two are used in lesser amounts and the third in quantity. Blue and yellow are harmonious but too dramatic when used equally with red. However, an arrangement would be pleasing if blue were used as a dominant color with a small amount of red and yellow, provided the values and intensities are varied. To study triadic color combinations, make a cardboard equilateral triangle to fit the color wheel, with points touching each primary. Superimpose it on the wheel. Place pin in center. Spin it around wheel, and its three points will touch triadic colors that are harmonious when used together.

Cool and Warm Colors. On the color wheel, to the left of green and including yellow-green, lie the warm hues: orange and red. They are warmer toward red-orange. To the right of green lie the cool colors: blue-green, blue, violet-blue, and violet. They tend to be cooler toward blue. Warm colors suggest fire, blood, sunshine. They are bright and gay, exciting, stimulating, positive, advancing, attention-attracting. Cool colors seem more remote. They are somber, restful, passive, subdued, negative, and are known as retreating colors.

Flowers of warm colors are best for evening use, as cool colors tend to lose their identity in artificial light. Warm colors in an arrangement are inviting when the day is cold, but on a hot day cool colors are more desirable. A bowl of green leaves or blue flowers, encountered on a hot day, is as refreshing as a cold limeade. In a small room, cool colors seem to push back the walls. Try white flowers in a line arrangement against green walls for this effect. In a large room for some gay occasion, choose red-orange and yellow flowers. Mass them in an arrangement. On a dark day a bowl of marigolds is as spirit-lifting as a fire in the grate. Warm colors, if dominant in an arrangement, will make any cool color introduced into it seem cooler. Conversely, cool colors, if dominant, will cause the warm colors to seem warmer.

Photo Russell Illig   *Fern Bowers Hunt*

FIG. 20. Three purple tree peonies were the inspiration for this arrangement. They provide the focal point of interest and become dominant in the design. The violet lilacs and wisteria provide filler or subordinate material for the composition. The purple glass container relates to the plant material, both in texture and color.

Reflections from bright colors are stronger than from dark or grayed colors, and increase or decrease in degree according to the amount of sunlight present.

An arranger should observe the fundamental principles of design when arranging colors: proportion, balance, dominance, subordination, rhythm, and unity.

Color in background should never be the same hue or intensity as the flowers placed before it. If the arrangement is light in tone, the background should be darker; if the arrangement is dark, then the background should be lighter in value. Cool, dull colors are best used for large areas. The atmospheric blue of sky is an excellent color for background, and few flowers cannot be used successfully against it. Light yellow is also pleasing as background, but gold is better because of its richness. Velvety, rich-textured flowers are harmonious with old gold. When using flowers of intense hue, place the arrangement against a grayed background, or use backgrounds with tone tints that are lighter than the flowers in the arrangement. Red placed against green is not a good combination, as these two colors seem to swim together. Red against blue is good; blue-violet, however, should be carefully modified with gray.

Balance in planning for color necessitates a reminder that certain colors seem to have more weight than others; red-blue has more weight than blue; orange more than yellow. A strong orange calendula will balance a larger area of light gray-blue forget-me-nots. A bright gold anther on an African violet will balance a larger area of dull-hued petals. This is known as the law of color areas.

Watch for balance. A dark-colored flower placed on one side of a median line may be balanced by two flowers in lighter color on the other side. Balance an arrangement by placing the heavier, darker colors near the base and center of an arrangement; then grade them upward and outward, fading to lighter to give the same feeling as diminishing line in a branch. Variations of value from dark to light make for interest and a feeling of stability.

The general law, as stated by A. H. Munsell in his valuable manual of color is that the "stronger the color we wish to employ, the smaller must be its area, while the larger the area, the grayer or weaker the chroma." Small bits of powerful color can be used to balance a large field of weak chroma. The Munsell Manual of Color explains in clear detail why warm colors come forward while cool ones recede, why warm colors are stimulating and cool ones more restful. Every student should read and try to understand this work.

Proportion in planning for color requires that there be a dominant hue in any arrangement, to key the flowers to their container and to set the mood you wish to convey.

Rhythm is found in repetition of color. It leads the attention through repeated colors, sequences from dark to light, and orderly sequence of adjacent hues and their tints and shades. Variation in orderly sequence of intense color is another means of showing rhythm.

Psychology of Color. It is a well-established theory that color has a psychological effect on people, and various colors have become associated symbolically with certain qualities, traits, and aspects of human life. The appropriate color in altar cloth and vestments is governed by the particular season of the church year. (See Color Connotation, Appendix IV). According to psychologists, the most popular colors, in the order named, are red, blue, violet, green, orange, yellow. (See also liturgical colors for High Altar in church calendar, Appendix VIII.)

❧ 5 ❧

Principles of Design and Their Application

There are many people who depend on their native ability to arrange flowers. You may have heard it said, "Why should Mrs. John Doe study principles of design when she has such a way with flowers?" It is true that many people who have had no training at all arrange flowers exceedingly well. You can, no doubt, cite instances in other fields where artists have won renown without having had the benefit of formal guidance. However, had an education in good design been possible, they might have reached even greater success and might also have avoided discouraging mistakes and a waste of time and expenditure. The study of the principles of design in floral composition offers a logical means of learning and teaching the rudiments underlying all visual art. These principles have endured through the ages. As applied to floral arrangement, they should be used as steppingstones, never as crutches. They teach you how to begin, what to do, and why. With a thorough grounding in them and with perseverance and patience, success is practically assured. Each arrangement becomes easier than the one before, and you will find yourself applying the basic principles of composition as automatically as you drive a car.

Floral decorations, especially in relation to one's church life, should be an inspiring and joyous endeavor. Arbitrary rules should not be allowed to stifle creative urge. Each arranger should feel free to express her own feelings and taste, within the limits of appropriateness and of church regulations. Arrangements composed with freedom of thought and originality of concept usually tend to be interesting and dynamic.

However, when it is suggested that a person should feel free to express his own taste, it should not be inferred that there need be no order in floral composition, for order is of the essence. Order is the law of the universe. It may be observed in the veining of a leaf, the arrangement of petals of a flower, the structure of the human body, the design of a shell or a snowflake. Unless there is order in the arrangement of a floral composition, the eye wearies from searching for a way into it, and a way out, just as it does from the effect produced by the haphazard placement of articles in a show window or in any untidy room.

The principles of floral composition are the stop-and-go signals of good design. They are proportion, scale, balance, dominance, subordination, rhythm, repetition, transition, and contrast and variety.

Proportion is the first principle to be considered because we must first establish the proportions of an arrangement before we can cut or place the plant materials for it. Marjorie Deverel, in her *Outline Study of Flower Arrangement*, defines proportion as "the aesthetic space relationship between the parts of a floral composition and its relationship to the space around it."

The ancient Greeks pondered long the subject of proportion and gave the world what is known as the golden section, or the oblong. They determined that the ratios of 2 to 3, 3 to 5, and 5 to 8 are more pleasing than absolutely equilateral sides in an object. They also learned that an ellipsoid is more interesting than a sphere, and a parallel-sided solid more beautiful than a square mass. The eye instinctively compares basic forms in objects. Nearly everyone has an innate sense of proportion. We usually know when an object is too wide or too high for the space it fills and are vaguely disturbed by this. Subconsciously we compare spaces and sizes in regard to their silhouette against a background space. Since the purpose of an arrangement is to please, certainly it must have pleasing proportions. The plant material must be proportionate to the container, and is usually cut one and one half times the width or height of the container, if it is to be a *mass* arrangement. If a *line* arrangement is planned, the plant material should be cut at least three to five times the height or width of the container, depending on the weight, color, and size of the flowers or on the delicacy or slenderness of the line material. Accentuation of long slender lines in plant material can give style to a room. Never crowd a background space or duplicate the height of the vase with that of the plant material. Use uneven sizes in flowers, un-

DESIGN

RATIOS 2X3, 3X5, & 5X8
ARE PLEASING FORMS FOR CONTAINERS

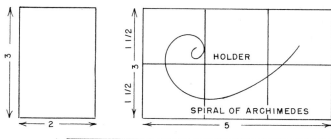

GOLDEN OBLONG

SHORT SIDE, 3/5 OF LONG SIDE, SHOULD BE DI-VIDED BETWEEN 1/2 AND 2/3 THE LENGTH AREA FOR FOCAL POINT.

HOLDER

SPIRAL OF ARCHIMEDES

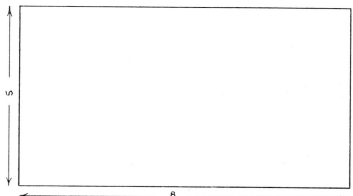

FOUR DIVISIONS OF DESIGN

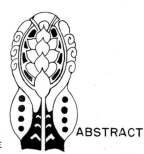

CONVENTIONAL

GEOMETRIC
PLANNED ONLY WHEN USING INANIMATE MATERIALS

ABSTRACT

NATURALISTIC DESIGN
FOLLOWS GROWTH HABITS OF PLANTS

SEE GLOSSARY

FIG. 21

Robert Miller

Photo Russell Illig   Fern Bowers Hunt

FIG. 22. The gray-green color of the robe of the hand-carved wooden figure of St. Francis ties harmoniously in color and line with the strong vertical lines of the agave leaf. Succulents are placed at the feet of the figure. Deodora boughs form a mat and balance the height and visual weight of the leaf, which has been used as an enclosure to set the figurine apart from other objects in the room.

even lines in stems, unequal numbers of each when composing an arrangement. Remember that the use of directional lines will carry attention beyond actual length of materials (especially if the plant materials taper and repeat themselves). Turn the tips of stems back if they are too long and if the arrangement seems to lose its balance.

A vertical arrangement looks best against a correspondingly vertical background, a horizontal one against a horizontal background. Learn from nature. Tall pines repeat the pyramidal shape of lofty mountain peaks, while the domelike form of spreading oaks repeats the contour of rolling foothills. An arrangement should never extend more than two thirds of the height or width of the background space. For a dining table, plan a low arrangement. The size and shape of the container and the size of the table will determine the size and proportion of the composition. No table arrangement should occupy more than one third of its surface space.

Scale, as Webster defines it, is the pleasing and consistent relationship of sizes without difference in proportion of parts. Large flowers look at home in large containers; small ones in small containers. Scale is the most important element when constructing miniature arrangements or when using a figurine. The bird in a simulated scene must not be larger than the sheltering "tree."

It is easier to suit the sizes of flowers to figurines of birds, fish, or very small animals than it is to suit them to figurines that depict humans or large animals. If you use figurines depicting humans as part of an arrangement, then you should use delicate plant materials, such as small grasses or very tiny flowers, that may be interpreted as likenesses of trees, etc. To maintain the feeling of imagery, try setting your arrangement apart from books, lamps, bric-a-brac. This may be done by placing a plaque, small screen, a large leaf, or other enclosing device behind it. (Consult list of "filler material" in Appendix VI, Selected Lists of Plant Materials.)

Symmetrical or asymmetrical balance must be established in any floral arrangement and is determined by the first placement of a stem.

Symmetrical balance conveys a feeling of dignity and repose. There is equal distribution of plant material on either side of a central placement. This establishes an axis where plant material meets container. Visually, each piece of plant material should balance and counterbalance the other as to weight, height, color, color value, texture, and spacing on either side of a centrally placed axis. Symmetrical balance is more static and less dynamic than asymmetrical, but it is

Photo Russell Illig   *Fern Bowers Hunt*

FIG. 23. A hand-carved Italian Madonna is placed before a palm spathe which forms a niche proportionate in size to the figure. Grandiflora Magnolia leaves, which show the reverse side, are placed in a rayed position, and deodora cone roses are placed at the feet of the figure. The container is a brown wooden Lazy Susan. A large heavy pin frog keeps the plant material in place. This is a study in symmetrical balance.

usually more appropriate and pleasing for altar arrangements. This is not to say that asymmetrical balance can never be employed in arrangements for the altar, but it should be used then in paired arrangements.

Asymmetrical balance is found when one side of an arrangement differs from the other in relation to the first placement. A large flower will counterbalance a long horizontal stem on the other side, if the stem is long enough. The eye will tell if the balance is correct. The first placement will, of course, establish the height of the arrangement. It should be placed off center in the container, and, in turn, the container should be placed off center on a mantel, chest, or table, unless pairs of arrangements are used on an altar. An interesting aspect of asymmetrical balance is the tension that develops from the vertical placement of plant material in an arrangement.

For instance, a vertical stem will appear taller and more imposing than in the horizontal placing of one exactly the same size, color, and texture. This optical illusion arises from a subconscious association we experience with respect to the law of gravity. Ernest Mundt, an eminent authority on design, illustrates this by stating that more tension and energy are involved when a man stands than when he lies down. Other things also influencing this type of balance in an arrangement are repetition and diminishing in lines, colors, textures, and forms—all of which will tend to lead the eye beyond actual dimension.

Radial balance is apparent in the simplest arrangements, in which one flower serves as the hub of a wheel, so to speak, and fan lines converge to the common center. If a few petals from a daisy used thus are missing, or a few spokes from a wheel, we feel the imbalance. A French nosegay is constructed on the principle of radial balance; when making one, be sure that each ring placement around the center is evenly placed and that each flower in each circle is approximately the same size.

Vertical balance is achieved by placing large forms low, deep colors low, wispy and airy light-colored materials high (compactness low, openness high). The size of the flowers used will be a determinant, also dark or light tonal color placement.

Dominance in an arrangement is achieved by placing an eye-catching feature near the point where axes cross. Dominance gives character and substance to an arrangement.

Subordination refers to the use of "filler" plant materials which

Photo William Arborgast   *Lillian Mund*

Fig. 24. *Wesley Methodist Church, Palo Alto, Calif.* Dark green loquot crescent-shaped branches effectively silhouette the white flowers of the chrysanthemums in various stages of bloom. The repetition of design in leafy branch and flowers emphasizes the symbolic significance of this lunar study.

Photo Burton Crandall *Fern Bowers Hunt*

FIG. 25. When flowers in the garden are few we may have to look to our house plants for material. This arrangement of pink geraniums and their leaves came from this source. The container consists of a Victorian cake plate and two silver compotes built up in tier formation. This arrangement would be suitable for a table, mantel, or desk.

RADIATION

FROM A
POINT

FROM A HUB OR
CENTER

FROM A CENTRAL
AXIS AS IN
GARLANDS

FROM A CURVE AS IN
A WREATH

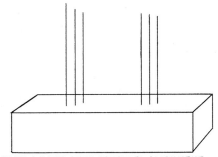

FROM A BASE AS IN PARALLEL ALIGNMENT

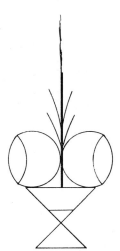

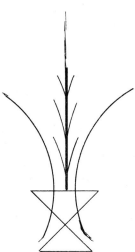

HYPERBOLOID DESIGNS

FIG. 26

Robert Miller

are subordinate to the dominant features but which give interest to the arrangement.

Rhythm is produced by repetition, by progression or diminution of lines, forms, colors, color values, and sizes. It may also be produced when the attention is led from one element to another in orderly sequence. Rhythm is the path *through* an arrangement and is often called its design. Rhythmic feeling can be achieved with broken lines, if they are directional and if the spaces between the breaks are not too great. Should you wish to effect a wind-blown, motile feeling, all flowers should be placed to face in the same direction.

Transition in floral arrangement is accomplished by using plant materials calculated to lead the eye gently from one color, line, or form to another. For example, a fruit arrangement for Thanksgiving might contain a watermelon and some grapes, but something in a transitional size between these two would be necessary, in order to tie them together harmoniously. A cantaloupe and some apples would be right for this (see tabular listing, p. 186).

Contrast makes for interest in an arrangement and sets it apart from background. Contrast your arrangement against a darker or lighter background or against a complementary color. This will provide a startling effect.

Variety is mentioned because variety in color, color value, texture, line, size, form, all add zest. But be warned! Too much variety is as bad as too little. Do not use too many different kinds of plant materials in a particular arrangement, or too many colors or textures. From three to five is a safe limit unless it is a mixed bouquet.

Radiation. We have discussed radial balance, and while radial design is akin to radiation, the two differ. Radiation may stem from a common center, as in the wheel; from a point, as the veining of a palmate leaf; from an axis, such as the veining outward from the midrib on a leaf; from a base, such as where the fingers and toes join the hand or foot; and radiation may stem from a curved line.

All these types produce interesting placements in the design of an arrangement. Try making hyperboloid designs using accessories.

Planning Floral Arrangements

In this section, consideration is given to a number of factors it is necessary to think about in planning floral arrangements in accordance with the principles of good design. The ideas set forth hold true for decoration of church, home, or public gathering place. Inspiration can

Photo Russell Illig

Fern Bowers Hunt

FIG. 27. This mass arrangement of red, pink, and white winter stock with pink clematis forming the focal point is suitable for an altar or table decoration. The silver container ties harmoniously with the color of the flowers.

come from innumerable sources in the living world, some of the unexpected and delightful; but whatever the reason, whatever the occasion calling for floral decoration, the first step is to have in mind a plan or general design.

The main types of arrangement are mass, line, line-mass, and parallel alignment. Choose the type best suited to the plant material at hand and the space it is to decorate, and follow that type consistently in planning the design. The shape, size, texture, and color of the background will influence your choice of container. Many churches have only one kind of container suitable for altar floral decoration, and, in general, the background space to be considered in this regard does not change.

Mass arrangements are excellent for use in a church, and more especially on the altar and various other places in the sanctuary, because their compactness of form and concentration of color can be viewed from a distance. This type gives a feeling of stability and formality. It can be used advantageously in church recreation rooms or church classrooms, for table decorations, weddings, evening occasions, and also out of doors, to accentuate and point up a setting. Flowers and fruit in different stages of development are appropriate for the altar, in massed design. When mass arrangements are made for recreation rooms, such accessories as shells, rocks, wood forms, and figurines may be employed with flowers and foliage to set a mood or tell a Bible story. The design for a mass arrangement should follow the general architectural style of the church whenever possible, and the dominant features within the arrangement itself can provide a link between this and the fixed background space before which the arrangement is to be placed. It should fit comfortably before its background, not seemingly to "bump its head" nor yet to appear lost in vastness. As I have said elsewhere, tall arrangements look best before vertical panels, hemispherical ones before semicircular arches.

I have mentioned in a previous chapter the basic geometric forms and variations and combinations of them. The variations are usually more pleasing than the basic forms because the eye wishes to see variety; thus, an ellipsoid is more interesting than a sphere, an elongated pyramid more arresting than a strictly equilateral one. Design ideas can be found in the shapes of trees, flowers, and parts of flowers, leaves, buds, and bracts. Whatever form one chooses to follow, it should be carried through consistently. The design should follow the contour of the container and give a sense of balance and good proportion. It should be harmonious in color, texture, size, and intangible "feeling" with its surroundings. On an altar, a flower arrangement should lead attention to the cross, not away from it.

Line arrangements are thought of as skeleton-like designs of slender branches or straplike leaves. This type of design should be planned for plain, unbroken background spaces. A figured design in dorsal cloth, reredos, or molding will interfere with the appearance of upsweep in line.

If long lines are emphasized and repeated in an arrangement, they may give a feeling of aspiration and may seem to raise the ceiling of a low room; if well spaced, to push back the walls. Vary length of stem lines and exaggerate them to gain style and show direction. Make sure there are no "stop signs" such as flat-headed flowers or crossed lines to impede visual progress or lead attention into a cul-de-sac. On page 184 you will find a list of plant material suitable for line arrangement, though it is never necessary to limit yourself to material found on any list.

FIG. 28. *Methodist Church, Los Altos, Calif.* A fall arrangement of chrysanthemums
for a contemporary style altar.

Curved lines are graceful and feminine in feeling. If used to excess, they may become tiresome. From a curved line may be evolved a spiral line arrangement, or a circular, concentric, vertical, horizontal, and a special type known as the Hogarth curve. An arrangement may also show combinations and variations of these. If you begin an arrangement with a curved line, continue it, repeat it, modify it.

Straight lines are visually fast, especially if they are narrow, are repeated, and taper at the ends. They impart a feeling of strength, severity, and formality. Variations such as zigzag and diagonal are lines of movement and force and are often as dramatic as a streak of lightning.

To give expression to lines, compare them as you would with lines of the body as they express mood and motivation. For example, bent and drooping lines in body position are expressive of defeat, dejection, the bent attitudes of age:

FIG. 29A

Uplifted lines show joy, elation, exaltation, aspiration, youth, happiness:

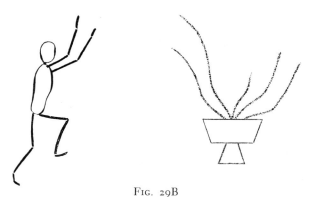

FIG. 29B

Horizontal lines are restful, express repose, inactivity, pause:

FIG. 30

Vertical lines express a feeling of uplift, aspiration, attention:

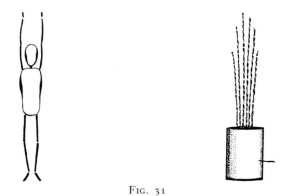

FIG. 31

Diagonal or zigzag lines express gaiety, are dramatic, can express action such as running, jumping, skiing:

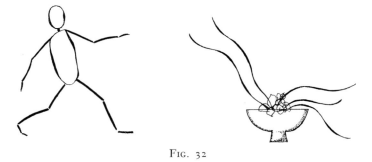

FIG. 32

Reverse curved lines are graceful, like a meandering stream:

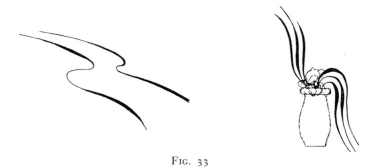

FIG. 33

Curved lines express the same circular, concentric feeling as in an animal curled in sleep. These lines return into themselves and are static:

Fig. 34

Spiral lines are graceful and expressive of lazy contentment, but are also uplifting lines. Smoke spiraling from a slow fire is analogous:

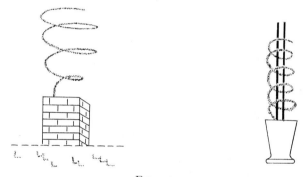

Fig. 35

Rayed lines, if symmetrical in fan shape, are dramatic in feeling, as are the rays of the setting sun:

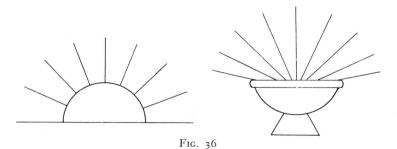

Fig. 36

Rayed lines in asymmetrical arrangement, particularly when long and narrow and when counterbalanced by short lines wide apart, are rhythmic and suggest motion:

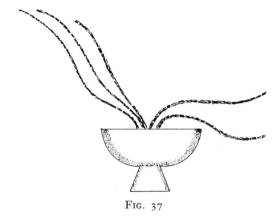

FIG. 37

Elliptical lines, if elongated, express aspiration, exaltation, triumph, as in arms raised above the head in exaltation:

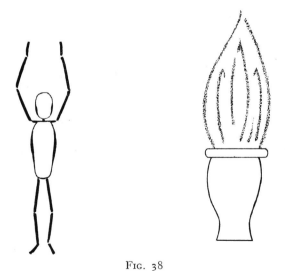

FIG. 38

Line arrangements are appropriate for small rooms and in places where they may be viewed at close range, but they are inappropriate for the altar.

A combination of *line* and *mass*, for convenience referred to as a mass-line arrangement, is the writer's preference. By employing the dynamic quality of line plant material and combining it with the charm of form in fruit or flowers, an arrangement gathers heightened interest, as this combination best affords opportunity to develop mood and feeling. If successful, a mass-line composition calls forth spontaneous response in the observer.

❧ 6 ☙

Choice of Plant Material

Blossoms and flowering branches
Lately from the sod—
Preface and introduction
To the manuscript of God.

A wealth of plant material is available to anyone with eyes to see, the desire to create, and a collector's instinct for securing long-keeping, beautiful plant materials, both fresh and dried, for use in arrangements. With a plan in mind, satisfying and lovely arrangements can be composed with flowers, fruits, grasses that will lift the spirit of the arranger and transport the spectator out of the humdrum of everyday living. A perceptive arranger will hunt for the unusual among house plants, trees, shrubs, grasses, and weeds, as well as flowers from florist or garden. Fortunate is the church establishment with garden resources or the arranger with a home garden or the gardens of friends from which to cull. Garden flowers require some care before cutting, if they are to be at their best and are to last beyond a few hours.

Directions for Cutting Garden Flowers

1. Water soil around plants at least four hours before cutting, so they will be holding a maximum of water.
2. Always cut flowers when they are coming into bloom—never on the wane.
3. Best time for cutting is evening or early morning.
4. Carry a pail of water into the garden. Add one half teaspoon of

76

plant hormone, Bloomlife or Floralife (to prevent shock), and place flowers immediately into water. Cut stems extra long, on a slant with a sharp knife.

5. Pound and char woody stems; also char stems that ooze a sticky substance. Place all cut plants in deep water in a *cool dark* place to "harden" for at least six hours before arranging.

6. Cut the stems again under water, as air bubbles often form and prevent capillary action up the stem.

7. Strip off lower leaves to prevent fouling water.

8. If flowers have wilted, place the stem ends in boiling water for a few minutes, protecting the heads from steam, then plunge into cold water. This is especially effective with roses.

9. In an artificially heated building, keep the humidity as high as possible. This can be done by keeping a low fire under a filled kettle or by placing a shallow pan filled with water over the heating outlet.

10. Keep arrangements away from drafts, direct sunlight, and furnace outlets.

11. Change water on arrangements daily, using bulbous turkey-baster to siphon out water.

12. Add charcoal to the water to prevent odor from plants such as stocks, daisies, and marigolds.

13. Scour used vases and rinse free of soap.

Prolonging the Life of Cut Flowers

A consumer's report gives valuable information on prolonging the life of cut flowers. It suggests that certain commercial products tested in laboratories have beneficial effects on various cut plant materials. These products may be purchased at a florist's shop.

Zinnias, delphiniums, carnations, larkspur, snapdragons, black-eyed Susan and chrysanthemums are helped with *Survival 77*. The report judged this the best all-round product. *Aladdin Magic Flower and Plant Vitalizer for Carnations* was proved best for asters and winter jasmine. It was also found to be better than plain *Aladdin* for carnations. *Floralife* was judged best for roses and forsythia.

These preparations should be used in the following proportions:

Survival 77—1 tablespoon to each quart of water.

Aladdin Magic Flower and Plant Vitalizer—1 heaping tablespoon to each quart of water.

Aladdin Magic Flower and Plant Vitalizer for Carnations—2 tablespoons to each quart of water.

Floralife—2 tablespoons to each quart of water.

Bloomlife Cut Flower Food—3½ tablespoons to each quart of water.

Research conducted at the University of Tennessee, under the direction of Richard Edwin Garth and Associate Professor Lowell F. Bailey, has indicated roses and carnations will last a day longer if a commercial antiseptic is added to water. Sharp & Dohme's S.T. 37 throatwash was used in the experiment in the proportion of slightly less than 1 teaspoonful of antiseptic to 1 pint of water. The flower stems were cleared of fungi and bacteria, thus allowing the water to travel upward. Carnations will last 5 days longer if sugar, alum, and iron oxide are added to the throatwash solution. However, neither snapdragons, gladioli, daffodils, tulips, or stocks responded to any treatment. It was found that roses last longer in a sugar solution even if the antiseptic is omitted.

Gardening with an Eye to Floral Arrangement

If you have a garden plot in your church grounds, a great variety of flowers and especially shrubs and trees can be grown to furnish material for floral arrangements. For altar use, you will need material that is adequate in length and flowers large enough to "carry" when arranged, and that will be clearly seen from all parts of the church. If garden space and leisure time are at a premium, you should plant things that will harmonize with your church's architectural style and with interior colors and textures. In any garden you will also want to choose a succession of bloom for fragrance. A few fragrant blooms in an arrangement for church adds a precious and unexpected quality to the visual satisfaction it affords. The list of plant materials in the Appendix (page 189) is by no means exhaustive, long as it is. Of course, choice must be governed by matters of climate, altitude, available space, maintenance help, and in planning a particular arrangement, by individual taste and requirements.

Trees. Trees of forest and garden offer the arranger an endless variety of material. They produce boughs, leaves, flowers, fruit, berries, seed pods, decorative roots and bark. Some change with the seasons, displaying a range of hue, shade, and tone of color suitable to any décor and appropriate for any occasion. Forest and garden, or cultivated, trees fall into two groups: needle-leaved and broad-leaved. The needle-leaved evergreens or conifers (cone-bearing) offer unlimited material, as they are available the year round and are plentiful

Photo Russell Illig　　　　　　　　　　　　　　　　　　　　　　*Fern Bowers Hunt*

Fɪɢ. 39. This colorful summer arrangement of pink roses and pale blue delphinium was inspired by an 18th-century religious painting. This bouquet is well suited to a traditional type church.

in high altitudes as well as along the seacoast. Arid regions also have their evergreens: juniper, cedar, yellow pine, pinon.

The needle-leaved evergreens are especially welcome in winter when flowers are few, and, of course, they take precedence over other material for decorative purposes during the Christmas season. Their delightful fragrance, redolent of the forest, is exhilarating when gaiety is in the air. Boughs of the pine family are unusually beautiful because their long-needled leaves lend grace to mantel decoration and use in

Photo William Arborgast   *Maude Smith*

FIG. 40. *Wesley Methodist Church, Palo Alto, Calif.* Dried gray-green hydrangeas harmonize with gray-green New Zealand flax in this contemporary type arrangement. It is free from clutter, and its aspiring lines reflect those of the architecture.

Photo Esther Wagner   *Fern Bowers Hunt*

FIG. 41. A cone swag for a window or above a mantel is effective during holidays. The cones are wired to hardware cloth and evergreen twigs are inserted between the cones into the wire. This type of decoration is suitable for either the traditional or the contemporary type church or church recreation rooms.

swags, garlands, and wreaths. The most dramatic of the conifers is the sugar pine, with its short needles and oversized cones, the latter sometimes reaching a length of 24 inches. Three of these cones on a feathery evergreen bough, tied with ribbon, make an attractive door swag. However, Christmas decoration is not the only purpose the evergreens serve. More and more they are being used through the year with various kinds of cut flowers.

A gracefully curved spray of dark pine, used with a few flowers such as yellow or bronze chrysanthemums in a copper bowl, takes the place of a massed arrangement of many flowers. Incense cedar, with its yellow cast, is very effective with the bright yellow of daffodils.

Broad-leaved trees are a great asset to the arranger, as their branches give stability and character to a composition. When flowers are few, the broad-leaved branches supplement this lack. A variety of leaves arranged without flowers is restful and pleasing, especially against a patterned background.

See facing page for legend.

Flowering trees can be planned for a garden so that flowering branches are available almost the year round. In my own Northern California garden, for instance, the feathery yellow acacia comes to flower in January. It is followed by ornamental flowering trees such as jacaranda and mimosa; the pink masses of locust blossom; the rose-pink of hawthorn; *magnolia soulangeana* (often mistakenly called the tulip tree) with its beautiful tulip-shaped flowers; the misty pink and white clouds of crab apple, plum, apple, pear, peach, and almond blossom. *Magnolia grandiflora*, an evergreen tree, with its large ivory-colored, waxy cups and long blooming season, carries through almost until the acacia begins another cycle. These are only a few of the trees providing material for church arrangements.

Trees native to an area, so-called wild trees, provide different effects for different seasons. If you cut alder when it is first coming into leaf and place the branches in deep water, they will last a long time. They may have little brown cones hanging on them from the year before; these are lovely with the new leaves. The alder in full leaf with its new crop of tiny green cones is beautiful when used in an arrangement. The cones may be used in wreaths and on gift packages.

In New England, the witch hazel comes into delicate golden flower while snow is still on the ground. The ever-popular pussy willow, cut late in winter or in early spring, will keep for a long time if arranged without water. In choosing graceful branches for an arrangement, look low on the trees for those that are curved from reaching toward the sunlight. Cork elm offers branches that are easy to manipulate and that last well in water; the rough gray bark is pleasing in a dark gray or pewter bowl.

Since forest trees are protected by conservation laws and cultivated trees belong to the people who cultivate them, you may find it advantageous to plant a few yourself, if possible. They add distinctive beauty to a garden and provide a constant source of decorative material.

City dwellers need not be entirely dependent on the florist for plant materials. There are many plants whose leaves and flowers lend themselves to interesting arrangements and that can be grown indoors; these can be pruned during the winter months, and when cut flowers

FIG. 42. *Stanford University Memorial Church, Stanford, Calif. Easter Service.* White tree azaleas growing in pots flank the white marble altar of this Byzantine interior. White rhododendrons and broad leaves of the camellia are used together in the decorations for the altar.

are scarce and expensive, and when neither garden nor countryside yields much, house plants alone can furnish material for ingenious and creative arrangements. The list on page 186 suggests many plants from which the city dweller can make a choice.

The simplicity and sense of space in modern, functional church interiors seem to call for the use of broad-leaved material. The leaves

Photo William Arborgast   *Fern Bowers Hunt*

Fig. 43. *Episcopal Church, Portola Valley, Calif.* Arrangements of white gladiolus and winter stock flank the altar of this contemporary type village church. A permanent planting of house plants is seen back of the altar.

of plants listed on page 186 will be found valuable in creating designs for contemporary backgrounds.

Fruit Arrangements

Fruits used decoratively can be practical as well as beautiful. Because of their simple forms they are easy to arrange, economical to use, and available the year round. Rapid transportation has blessed us with a wide variety of imported and domestic fruits which come to us in excellent condition, thereby providing great scope in planning fruit arrangements. There are fruits for very occasion and to enhance every color scheme. Carefully chosen, they may harmonize perfectly with vestments, linens, and altar adornments. Fruit arrangements are appropriate for luncheon or dining tables in church recreation rooms and are effective wherever a floral arrangement would be. They can be contemporary or traditional in feeling, thus increasing their versatility.

Whenever fruits are used, they must be completely fresh and free of blemish; and, of course, as with any other plant material, the elements of good design must be followed in their arrangement. A fruit arrangement offers nourishment to both body and soul, since it can be eaten after the arrangement has served its purpose.

Expensive containers are not necessary in such compositions. Plaques, leaves, mats, hollow gourds, palm sheaths, or driftwood are not only suitable but beautiful. If no container is to be used, place foil on table to protect it, and over this place leaves in a harmonious color. As an example, the underside of an avocado leaf is the same gray-green as the leaves of the pineapple. Ti or aspidistra leaves make an attractive foundation when placed under fruits. The leaf of the prickly pear cactus, cut from the parent plant with a sharp knife and the spines removed with crumpled newspaper, makes a unique container for fruit. It has excellent keeping qualities and is contemporary in feeling. In Fig. 44 the green of the leaf complements the yellow of the grapefruit, which is used as a center of interest. The three bananas, arranged to show direction of line, are harmonious in color and tie the green lemons to the cactus leaf. A sprig of euonymus, in yellow and green, is used for accent.

This pyramidal arrangement is a simple way to teach the beginner how to group objects.

When you arrange fruits, select a dominant form and follow its line direction. As shown in Fig. 44, the bananas take the same curve as the grapefruit. The eye may be led pleasantly through an arrangement by using fruits of harmonious color placed in orderly sequence. The

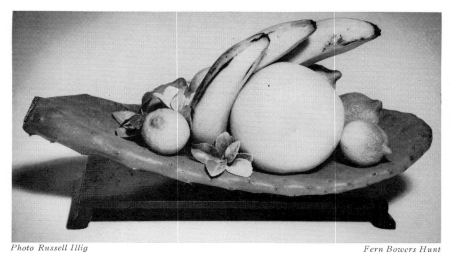

Fig. 44. Pyramidal arrangement of fruit in a natural container. (See text.)

diminishing ends of grapes and leaves are pleasing when placed near the outer perimeter. Bananas give height by their slim vertical appearance.

Flowers may be kept fresh when combined with fruit by inserting small pickle jars or orchid tubes or grapes concealed with leaves. The stem of a leaf will draw moisture and sustenance from a grape. Such flowers as gardenias, camellias, or tuberous begonias may be combined with fruit, in an arrangement, without placing them in water. Keep in mind color harmony when combining several kinds of fruit: for instance, apples, red or yellow oranges, bananas, cherries, lemons, tangerines, apricots, peaches, persimmons, kumquats, loquats, pineapples, and green grapes together. You might also group cool colors, such as blue plums, blue, purple, or green grapes, eggplants, lemons, nectarines, cherries, guavas, and pomegranates.

Purple, deep-blue, red and yellow-green fruits and vegetables are another harmonious grouping. Fruits that go well together are pineapple, apricots, guavas; avocados, apples—either red or yellow, Royal Anne cherries; red plums, loquats, dark-red Bing cherries; blue plums, cherimoya, green apples. The gray-green of the guava is harmonious with the gray-green of pineapple leaves, green grapes, and oranges.

Grasses, Sedges, Reeds, and Rushes (*Wild and Cultivated*)

In the constant search for new and interesting materials for decoration, the arranger with vision and imagination should turn to highway and byway, field and stream for the unusual. Grasses, sedges, reeds, and rushes will be found in vast profusion. Indeed, these plants are so satisfactory they may be worth while to grow in your garden. Before going into their decorative uses, it is well to give a few simple ways of differentiating between them.

Grasses include the family of cereal grains, both wild and cultivated. Wild grasses are found along streams and in marshes, also in arid regions. A single leaf appears at each joint, alternating on opposite sides of the stem. Timothy and bluegrass belong in this family. Cereal grasses or grains include barley and wheat, both tufted and plain; rice, oat, and rye; when cultivated and grown specifically for decoration, these are more desirable than wild oats, etc. It is interesting that cereal grains do not reseed themselves prolifically, but need man's help in propagation.

Rushes and sedges are often mistaken for each other, as they both grow in moist places, but on examination (and in most cases) you will find the stems of sedges are solid and are not enlarged at the joints. Rushes and sedges are very similar in appearance, but the stems of rushes are hollow. Among these are long-leaf rush and Western rush.

Reeds also grow along streams and in marshy places. They have fibrous, running root stalks which make them valuable in preventing soil erosion. Some reeds have tufted panicles that hang down like bushy grass, such as the common reed and the giant reed. Others have upstanding tufts, such as cattail. Of the reeds, these latter, both large and small, are much sought after by arrangers because of their dramatic appearance.

Grasses, rushes, sedges, and reeds may be used decoratively either in their green state or dried. Because of their simple forms and pliability, they are easy to arrange, and since they last indefinitely, economical to use. See page 195 for a list of grasses that are widely distributed, not protected by law and that may be had for the taking, unless, of course, the land is posted. If you wish grasses to retain their beautiful coloring, they must be cut in the green state before they reach maturity. Especially is this true of grains, to keep the kernels from dropping.

Photo Russell Illig

Fern Bowers Hunt

FIG. 45. Thanksgiving arrangement of bearded barley and oats is suitable for a church recreation room. The quail is life-sized and repeats the color and texture of the cereal grain. Geranium leaves are placed low in the composition to tie the plant material to that of the figurine and to cover the pin frog.

Since dried grasses are difficult to transport, it is wise to choose materials indigenous to one's home region or to grow one's own. Grasses are the easiest of all plants to grow, as they mature much more quickly than flowers and there are varieties for every soil and location. Their colors are harmonious in any surrounding and their individual designs are exquisitely beautiful. They may be used in closely massed effect (tied together) or as airy "filler-in." Try using a magnifying glass to study individual stalks. You will find exquisite and interesting designs and color harmonies that are beautiful and rare, that may help you in design.

When these plant materials are dried, they may be used in winter bouquets and are a boon to one living at a high altitude, on the desert, or where winter flowers are few. This kind of arrangement may be depended on for about nine months of the year. As with flowers and fruits, only grasses free from blemish and in good condition should be used in arrangements. Spiky grasses and reeds look best when placed high, and those with rounded heads are best used at center and low in the composition. Containers which have an affinity for these materials are driftwood, baskets, hollowed-out juniper roots, unglazed pottery, brass, pewter, and copper.

Mention is made of only those grasses that are widely distributed, easy to obtain, exceedingly decorative and that will not become pests in a garden should their seeds be scattered.

Care of Grasses

The following simple rules are useful when working with grasses:

To clean: Immerse in lukewarm water.

To dry: Hang upside down in a dark place. Grains should be dried right side up. Make small separate bunches of one kind.

To keep from dust: Drape cheesecloth around material after it has been dried.

To shape: If you wish to reshape grasses for arranging, place them in warm water for a half hour; bend gently over a rounded object such as a coat hanger bent to the desired shape; tie and allow to dry.

To arrange: Plan an arrangement when grasses are still green. Place them in a dry container in which they are to remain. As in any other type of arrangement, consider principles of good design.

৯৯ 7 ৯৯

Backgrounds, Containers, Accessories

As a jewel is improved by a setting and a painting by a frame, so does a flower arrangement need an appropriate background to enhance its beauty of line and color. Background is definable as the space behind an arrangement. There should be no design on it to vie with or detract from the plant materials used in the arrangement.

In most churches, the background before which arrangements may be placed is fixed, and especially is this so around the chancel and altar; but this need not be a restriction, and there are many other places, as well, in church rooms where floral arrangements can be most effectively used decoratively. Since walls are permanent, and, with respect to the altar, dorsal cloths and reredos must be dealt with, we sometimes find them out of harmony with some effect we wish to create. In this case, it may be necessary to modify one's arrangement to suit one's purpose. For example, after completing an arrangement, try placing large, broad leaves in the container to act as a background.

The simplest Japanese home provides a special place for flower arrangements, called a *tokonoma*. An alcove, a plain wall area, or an undecorated piece of matting of good proportion hung on a wall, the *tokonoma* becomes the focal point of the room and provides the proper setting for an arrangement. We, too, should provide, wherever possible, a satisfactory background for an arrangement of special beauty—except, of course, in areas of the sanctuary where anything added would be inadmissible. A cloth hanging of plain harmonizing color and texture, mounted on poles of bamboo or other wood, may be used. The material may be velvet or satin for a formal setting or one of rougher homespun material for a less formal one. Screens may also be utilized to block out or change a background. Paneled walls of wood make beautiful backgrounds for contemporary driftwood arrangements.

Conceivably, figured wallpaper might be used in certain church social rooms, posing a problem for the sensitive arranger. A permanent plain background for floral arrangements can be made by paneling an area with narrow molding, then covering the enclosed wall space with plain paper the exact hue of the predominant hue in the wallpaper. The panel must be carefully proportioned; as stated previously, the ratios of two or three, three to five, and five to eight are most satisfying.

A mirror may be used as a background for an arrangement. It is particularly effective if you wish to lighten a room or create an illusion of greater size. When few flowers are available, a mirror seemingly will multiply the number used in an arrangement. Plaques and large trays may also be used to provide a pleasing background.

Backgrounds should be subdued in color. Grayed or neutral colors are good, as a wide range of plant material may be used against them. If you wish to use strong colors in an arrangement, avoid very light or washed-out backgrounds. For a restful feeling use grayed colors in both background and arrangement.

If the walls are strong in color, an understanding of good color harmony can produce lovely effects with flower arrangements. Flowers of one color alone may be used, or green leaves in various sizes, shapes, textures, and values, omitting any flowers. Bright flowers of harmonizing colors may be used against a bright wall if there is enough grayed foliage to neutralize their intensity.

Containers and Accessories

When acquiring containers for your church, choose them not for their intrinsic value as works of art but for their main purpose, the holding of flowers. Although a vase may be priceless, it is not always desirable as a flower container. The Portland vase in the British Museum is considered one of the most exquisitely beautiful in the world. It was designed by the Romans in the first century as a funerary urn; but its narrow neck, bulging sides, and decorated surface make it (or a modern counterpart) inappropriate as a flower container.

While the container is important in any floral composition, it should not take precedence over the plant material. When paired containers are used on the altar, they should of course be subordinate to the cross. A container is not a sacred vessel and is not blessed.

The container is an integral part of any good floral decoration. It should be in harmony with background, with whatever supports it, and with the material it holds. Also, it should be functional—large enough to hold sufficient water to keep the plant material fresh and deep enough to hide the mechanics of maintaining the material in place. The basic forms found in containers are cubes, spheres, cones, cylinders, pyramids, and variations and combinations of these. The best ones are simple in line, undecorated, and subdued in color. The base should be large enough to convey the impression of roots spread out.

The Orientals learned that certain flower arrangements are enhanced by placing the container on a base or stand. The reason for this is that in a basic form such as an inverted cone or a pyramid, the form cannot be complete because of necessity the container must have a flat bottom. However, the eye *wishes* to see the form complete, and if a base or stand is placed under the container, the eye is able to imagine the entire shape; the eye would picture the apex of an inverted cone touching at the table line, below the footed stand. This is known as "occult balance." (See page 43.)

It cannot be said too often that plant material in an arrangement should look as if it were growing naturally. It is well to choose containers with this idea in mind. The lines of an arrangement should follow the contour of the container, and since most plants grow in an upward and outward manner, vases and bowls with flaring tops are preferable to those that cup inward. If you must work with such a shape as the latter, the flowers and foliage should be brought down over the rim to conceal the "cupping-in."

Vertical-sided containers would be effective in a church of contemporary style, and these have a special affinity for iris, members of the narcissus and lily families, cattails, bamboo, and other plants which grow in an upright manner and look their best when arranged that way. Wide-mouthed containers are used for mass arrangements. A narrow-necked vase is often employed for single-stemmed or few-flowers.

When choosing flower containers, it is wise to give some thought to both the architectural style of one's church and to the kind of social life carried on in its social rooms; whether the emphasis is on formal or informal gatherings (or a little of each); whether the church and its subordinate meeting rooms are traditional or contemporary in furnishing. But do not be too rigidly bound in your thinking; many churches blend elements of many periods and many styles in the furnishing of these rooms.

Good proportion and relation in scale to surroundings are necessary in the choice of a container. Since plant material is usually cut at least one and a half times (or more) the height or width of the container to be used, the space it is to occupy may be calculated with a yardstick. This should be done *before* beginning to assemble the arrangement. It behooves the arranger to choose a container that will set the proper proportions for the chosen area and to see that adequate space surrounds it—just as in hanging a picture on a wall. Altar containers must, of course, be in harmonious relationship with the cross and candlesticks. There should be no surface embellishments on the container. However, if there are enrichments of line that conform to the contour, these serve to give rhythm and interest to the piece. The enrichment should seem to grow out of the body of the container, and simplicity should be the keynote in the design of the arrangement placed in it.

A well-chosen container can emphasize the mood you wish to convey. There should also be some relationship between different containers placed in a church gathering room. In a room of average size, one large container and two smaller ones, related in color, texture, and feeling should give good balance. Again we learn from the Oriental custom of displaying a few fine objects (or arrangements) at a time. Of course, a special occasion such as Easter, a feast day, or floral decoration for a wedding may call for more lavish display.

Texture, the quality of roughness or smoothness in a material, is not to be neglected in the selection and use of containers. There should be harmony of texture between container, contained, and background. You would not place a formal arrangement of plant material in a fine silver bowl on a rough-hewn, unpolished altar in a rustic church, nor a driftwood arrangement on a marble altar.

Color is important in a container and must be chosen to blend with the plant material, the background, and the spot on which the whole composition is to rest. The container's color may be deeper than the predominating colors in the plant material, or it may be

FIG. 46. Red roses and bleeding heart arranged in a pewter bowl is a pleasing composition for a Valentine party.

the same, and pick up its hues. Grayed or muted color in bowls and vases are pleasing, as they tend to blend in tone with the stems and leaves of many growing materials.

Value, the relation of color to black and to white, is another factor to consider in containers. Those light in value seem to come forward, the darker ones to recede. The container should seem to melt into whatever supports it.

The kind of lighting in a church, whether artificial or natural, will also play a part in selection. Materials like silver, brass, and certain highly glazed pottery reflect light and will often distract attention from the flowers or plant material in the arrangement. Pewter is often more satisfactory than silver, and unpolished brass (excepting altar pieces) and copper are excellent when used with flowers of harmonious hue. If a composition is to be placed on a dark altar or table, a dark-toned container would be suitable; if a light-finished piece is to provide support, a container light in value would be more appropriate.

Collecting containers can turn out to be a fascinating hobby for churchwomen and homemakers, and a lucky find may appear in the most unexpected place. Suitable containers may be of great monetary value or may cost little or nothing. Among the most versatile is the Oriental celadon gray-green rice bowl. Its form is excellent, it is inexpensive, and may be purchased wherever Chinese goods are sold. My own favorite container, unusually adaptable in many ways, has a copper base overlaid with pewter. It has a tendency to take on and reflect the colors of flowers placed in it, the copper tones predominating when autumnal shades are used; whereas when lavender, pink, and blue flowers are arranged in it, the pewter predominates and the vase harmonizes with these softer tones.

Sources of manmade containers for recreation rooms of a church are practically limitless and a great outlay of money to acquire appropriate and beautiful ones is hardly necessary. Miners' pans in three sizes are inexpensive and available in many hardware stores in the West. Their design is good, and they seem to take on the tone and color of whatever is placed in them. China and porcelain, from finest bone to colorful peasant pottery, as well as glass in all its variety, from delicate old Venetian and Bohemian pieces to modern imported or domestic ones, offer innumerable possibilities for holding flowers, provided the design is simple and functional.

If a glass container is transparent, plant stems should be carefully arranged under water and the holder concealed from view. This may be accomplished by using a smaller container of some opaque material inside the glass one, or by hiding mechanical aids with pebbles, shells, or marbles.

Baskets should be used in an informal manner and would go well in the parish hall of a rustic church. They are appropriate for wildflowers, fruit, and strong-bodied flowers like calendulas and strawflowers. They are pleasant with light-colored furniture and tawny shades so much in vogue.

Roadside, river bed, seashore, mountain area, and desert waste teem with beautiful natural materials appropriate as containers and accessories. Collection of them would be a praiseworthy effort in connection with a church bazaar. Rocks, shells, driftwood, and other beau-

Photo William Arborgast   *Fern Bowers Hunt*

FIG. 47. *Woodside Village Church, Woodside, Calif.* Lavender iris, rhododendron, and purple cinerarias were used to decorate the altar, of this traditional type church, for a spring wedding.

tiful forms may be had for the taking and, when used with discretion and taste, can provide a distinguished element in floral design.

Combinations of two or more related containers, built up in tier form, are satisfactory for receptions and when one needs to make few flowers look like many. This is also a very good way to use camellias, gardenias, tuberous begonias, and fruits in arrangements. A stemmed compote placed inside another stemmed dish, fastened with florist's clay and resembling the tiered cake plates of another day, can be successfully used as a container.

Harmonizing Container and Contained

After you have decided on the appropriateness of a particular container for a particular arrangement, it is a good idea to take it into the garden, if possible, to harmonize its color and texture with growing plant material. You will be surprised to see how well it will blend with a great many plants you may not have thought of using. Or you can reverse the order and bring the plant materials to the container shelf, holding them close to various ones to try for color harmony. Remember that artificial light, shadows, tone of background (wall or screen) will modify a container's color.

Bronze is much sought after for arranging flowering branches or pussy willows, as their stems are often bronze in color. Since it is always desirable to minimize the rim-line of the container, if the branches are close in tone, this is more easily accomplished.

Pottery in dull finish is excellent when used with strong-bodied flowers and leaves. Look for containers with earth tones—leaf green or green flecked with brown.

Brass is best used with green leaves but is also especially pleasing with yellow flowers, especially yellow-green. Many altar vases are brass.

Copper looks well with warm-colored flowers: red-orange, orange, orange-yellow, burnt orange, salmon, henna, peach, gold, yellow, rust.

Silver and pewter look best when used with cool colors: pink, mauve, heliotrope, purple, violet, blue.

Figurines and Accessories

For arrangements in church social rooms, also in work with children, the judicious use of figurines and other accessories can be very effective. At the risk of seeming to cast aspersion on certain of my readers' cherished notions, a word must be said about restraint in the use of both containers and accessories—the latter in particular. Just

Photo William Arborgast   *Fern Bowers Hunt*

Fig. 48. *First Congregational Church, Palo Alto, Calif.* A fan palm and olive branches were used in this radiating design to decorate the altar on Palm Sunday.

Photo Russell Illig   *Fern Bowers Hunt*

FIG. 49. An American handmade figurine of St. Francis dominates this interesting composition of eucalyptus seedpods and leaves. Careful attention to scale and to principles of figure portraiture are followed. The colors range from warm beige to yellow brown. This arrangement would be suitable for the children's department of a church or for a niche in the church recreation room.

because you may have been given a hollow china cow or somehow
have acquired an overdecorated maiden in bouffant skirt and wide
hat, with a hollowed-out portion of her lap made to hold blossoms,
it does not necessarily follow that such an object must be employed
in an arrangement in preference to the simple oval or rectangular
bowl or dish. Far too often, in bazaars and flower shows, the effect
of a carefully work-out arrangement is hopelessly marred by the addition of a figurine or other accessory neither appropriate nor harmonious with other elements of the composition. This impulsive addition can give the whole study an effect of cuteness. On the other
hand, an accessory truly harmonious in design, proportion, blending
or contrasting color, and above all having unity with the composition
under consideration, can provide the distinctive element that lifts
the whole thing above the commonplace and brings immediate
response from the observer.

Like a good container, a figurine or other accessory must be well
designed—in fact, it must be more than that. The container is an essential part of an arrangement but should be subordinated to the
plant material it holds. This is not true of a figurine: it must not
only dominate, it must take precedence. Never use a figurine unless
it is of good enough design to allow it to form an integral part of
the arrangement in respect to color, scale, appropriateness, and intangible feeling. This is not to say the color must be exactly the same,
but it must blend. Scale is equally important in working with figurines, to avoid a jarring sense of disproportion.

The plant material should be placed to follow the lines of a figurine, just as it does those of the container. For this reason, container
and figurine should be in perfect harmony. The figurine must complement and enhance the whole composition; if you are unsure, leave
it out. Shun so-called "cute" figures, be they elves, animals, or fac-
simile humans. Shiny, harsh, strong-colored ones are likewise no asset
in an arrangement, but if a particular object is fitting in every other
way, a too shiny surface can be toned down somewhat by dipping the
figurine in buttermilk or soapsuds and allowing it to dry.

✂ 8 ✂

Creating a Floral Arrangement

Up to this point we have considered the principles that are the foundation stones for the composition of floral arrangements—the laws that govern the art, the necessity for working with a purpose and plan, the relation of backgrounds, containers, and accessories to plant material, making a harmonious whole. With this firm grounding in the "why" of good floral arrangement, the amateur flounders between an occasional success and a dozen failures. But theory without practice is barren; it is like an overture without the drama.

The pleasantly exciting moment comes when all preparations are complete and you are ready to create a floral arrangement for your church. Perhaps you have been asked to arrange the altar flowers, or to produce the floral decoration for some church social occasion or special event; you may have been called on to decorate for a wedding. No matter—the procedure, the "how" of constructing a floral arrangement that will express what you want to communicate will be fundamentally the same. A number of ideas mentioned here I have dealt with elsewhere in this book, but they are brought together for convenience of the reader in following, step by step, the order of method in the creation of good floral arrangements.

If you plan one for a church of traditional style, you have probably chosen plant material and container suitable for a mass or mass-line arrangement. If, however, the setting is in functional-contemporary style, then you may have planned to do a line arrangement. In this case, you will do well to follow the trend of simplicity practiced by present-day architects and home decorators. Distortion has no place in floral arrangement worthy of its name. So, to be honest with materials and design, an arranger should place plant material after its natural manner of growth.

Choosing the Container

After you have decided on the type of arrangement to make, and before actually cutting plant materials, measure the background space with a yardstick (unless, of course, you are familiar with its proportions). In proportion, color, texture, quality and feeling, container and accessories, if any, should be in harmony with the background space and in scale with each other. No arrangement (after completion and including container and base) should extend more than two thirds the height or width of the background space. Interesting proportions—say, ⅓ to ⅔, are better than an equal division. On a table, an arrangement should occupy no more than a third of the surface area.

After looking over the supply of plant material in the garden, florist shop, or wayside, go over containers in your mind, with careful consideration as to their usability with whatever is available to arrange. Choose one with regard to the horizontal or vertical aspect of the background. If possible, take the container into the garden and hold it near plants you plan to use. Look carefully at stems, bracts, and the underside of leaves for colors that are harmonious. Consider scale and texture.

Choosing Plant Material

There are four main types of plants for line, mass, and mass-line arrangements: upright spear (delphinium, lupin, snapdragon, gladiolus, etc.); spherical and disc form (rose, camellia, dahlia, etc.); pendant (honeysuckle, fuchsia, grapes, etc.); filler-type (forget-me-not, syringa, gypsophila, etc.).

For line arrangements there are the whiplike branches from trees, shrubs, tall grasses, and strap leaves. For parallel alignment arrangements there are plants that grow vertically on stiff, strong stems, such as cattails, iris, etc. Plant material lists in the Appendix are useful in choosing materials for the kind of composition you plan.

Decide on colors for the proposed arrangement. If the occasion is an evening affair, cool colors will not be as satisfactory under artificial light as warm colors. Make sure fluorescent lights do not destroy your colors. To avoid this, choose colors that hold up under such lights, or if possible, use daylight-corrected light globes. For color and texture harmony, it is often helpful, though not always possible, to take a swatch of material the color of runners, dorsal cloth, or draperies into the garden and hold it near certain plants. You may find colors blending you might not otherwise have considered.

If you are fortunate in having access to a church garden planted with an eye to providing material harmonizing with vestment colors, you will usually find flowers and other plants that are right. Don't overlook flowering trees and shrubs for an ample supply. Rocks and woodforms indigenous to the area make valuable accessories for recreation rooms. The lichens and mosses that adhere to them will usually blend with other plant material.

Pre-Care

Every arranger should know something of the keeping qualities of cut plants and their natural habits of growth, and should learn to arrange them accordingly.

Remember to cut stems longer than you will need. Cut in the cool of the day, preferably after plants have been thoroughly watered and have drunk their fill. Except for a few annuals, morning is the best time for cutting. Choose buds and flowers coming into bloom, never those on the wane. Watch for plants showing interesting lines, those that reach for the light. Put cut material into deep water and place in a dark, cool place to "harden" for at least four hours. Use commercial preservatives. Pound woody stems and burn those that ooze a milky substance.

Step-by-Step Procedure

It is a good idea to arrange plant material at a site near the place it is to occupy. If this is not convenient, use any suitable table covered with a plastic or other type of groundcloth. It is well to place a second plastic cloth on the floor to protect it from water and cuttings. Segregate plant material as to height and color.

Have container and tools ready at hand. If you have a Lazy Susan, place the container on it so that as you arrange, it may be turned from side to side without disturbing the contents. The container should be slightly below eye level during this process, and if possible, you should sit while constructing the arrangement. Make sure you have light at your back and sides, never directly in front—otherwise colors in plant materials might be distorted.

Review your plan in your mind's eye. Consider how each flower, stem, and leaf has significance in your composition. However, in the process of actual creation, rules should take second place. Concentrate on the idea you yourself want to express. Use no more material than necessary to carry out that idea. The pattern you employ should follow any one of the basic forms: cylinder, sphere, cone, pyramid, or cube. Line patterns may be vertical, horizontal, oblique, circular, crescent, triangular, or the graceful Hogarth curve. There should be harmonious repetition of your dominant form or line as well as harmonious blending of color and texture.

Mechanical Aids

The proper choice of flower-holder is important. A pin frog, for instance, is best for a line arrangement; a basket pin holder for massed arrangements. Holders of the hairpin or ribbon type are also excellent. Heavy pin holders are a necessity for line arrangements.

Begin by stripping off all lower leaves on plants that will appear under water. If stems of a line arrangement are too fine to impale on a pin holder, wire a piece of woody stem to them. Slender stems may be bunched together or held with small elastic bands.

The Japanese have a type of holder called a *kubari*. This is merely a forked stick to hold stems. The arranger holds flowers in the left hand. A pliable cane about 4 inches long is wedged around the stems. The bent form of the cane leans against the rim of the container and holds the flowers in the desired position.

Suitable mechanical aids and good tools are as necessary to the art of floral arrangement as to any other art. A place where these can be assembled and kept at hand is one of the basic requirements for successful work. This may be a single shelf or a cupboard, or it may be a complete workshop stocked with the all-inclusive list of materials recommended on page 161.

For a **deep opaque container,** shape rabbit wire ½ inch mesh into a loose roll and insert into container, allowing about 2 inches to protrude above the rim-line of the container so that you can poke stems into the mesh at an angle. If there is danger of scratching the container, wrap the wire in aluminum foil before using. Rabbit wire may also be used to hold candles in place. Wrap the wire around a candle and then impale it on a pin holder. The wire must extend about an inch beyond the bottom of the candle and into the pinholder.

To elongate stems, splice them onto another stem with wire. Another way is to insert a short stem into an orchid tube and then wire the tube to a sturdy stem. Leaves and flowers must be arranged to conceal the mechanical device, and all trace of the artificial aid concealed.

A **deep transparent glass container** requires that an organized appearance of stems under water be presented; to do this, hold stems in left hand, keep stems close together, impale on pin holder *outside* the container. The pin holder should be large enough to hold the stems you wish to use in an arrangement. When stems are shaped to follow lines of the container, impale on the pin holder. Place plasticine in dry container where you wish to set the impaled stems. You may miter stems and lean them against the sides of the container. Cellophane tape will hold material to the rim-line. Grasp the tape in the center, wrap it once around the stem, and then tape both ends close together on the rim. Hide the tape with leaves.

Anchor a basket-type holder with florist's plasticine in a dry container. Press the holder down and give it a half-turn. Anchor a suction-type holder in a wet container. Use Posey clay for silver and fine metals. Fill your container with water before placing plant material in it.

Creating the Design

For a line arrangement, cut primary stem 1½ to 5 times or more the height or width of the container. Your proportions will depend on slimness of the material, weight of container, and, of course, height of background space. For a mass arrangement, cut primary stems 1½ times the height or width of the container. Cut them 1½ to 3 times the height and width of container for a mass-line arrangement. Place the primary stem first to establish type of balance and to conform to the container shape and to background space. This beginning framework will determine the final form of the composition. Continue to build your framework. You need only a skeleton form now; details will come later.

After the primary stem is placed, stand back and squint. A competent artist always backs away from his work in order to gain perspective, and squints to block out intrusive surroundings.

Choose slender material for line arrangements. Remember that straight lines are usually more formal than curved ones. In a line arrangement, what you leave out in plant material is probably as important as what you put in.

For mass or mass-line arrangements, spike forms should be placed at the outer perimeter and near the focal center. Rounded forms should occupy the middle ground, and pendant ones near the rim of the container. The design should grow outward by easy stages from the established axis where a dominant feature is used. This dominant material, along with filler material, creates a rhythmic path through the arrangement for the eye to follow.

Arrangements for the Altar

Mass or mass-line arrangements are the most satisfactory for placement on the altar of a church. The compactness of design and concentration of color in them afford greater carrying power when seen at a distance than do line or parallel alignment ones. However, each flower used should show to advantage. It is important to choose spike, spherical, and transitional (filler) plant materials for altar decoration in both the traditional and contemporary style of church architecture; broad leaves and flowers simple in form are very effective in a contemporary church setting. In considering color, harmony with vestments and other altar and general church furnishings is important. Colors lying in close juxtaposition on a color wheel and with similarity of intensity are the most pleasing because of their relatedness. It will set an altar arrangement apart to have it contrast with the background space; but within the arrangement itself, if colors or color values too strong in contrast with one another are used, the arrangement will appear to be full of holes when viewed from far back in the church (see Liturgical Altar, page 6).

One arrangement may be used on an altar when the cross is suspended above the altar and there is no tabernacle on it. The arrangement is centered on the gradin (raised ledge or step back of the altar) below the cross and is flanked by candlesticks.

Paired arrangements are usually used when the cross is centered on the gradin. They are placed on either side, equidistant, and each mirrors the other in material, size, color, color value, and design of curving or straight stems. The floral arrangements may flank the cross, with candlesticks and candles at the ends of the altar gradin, or the order may be reversed, with the floral decorations at the ends of the gradin. If more than two candlesticks and more than two arrangements are used, they may be placed to alternate with one another.

Paired arrangements must be alike in silhouette, so fruit and flower materials must be acquired in pairs insofar as possible. Stems must be alike in length, but curved ones must be in reverse in order to match. Before beginning the construction of the arrangements, background space should be measured for height and width, in order to make sure that plant material of sufficient length of stem will be provided.

The containers should be alike, also the mechanical aids used in building the arrangements. A heavy pin frog placed in the bottom of each vase and a loose roll of chicken wire impaled on it and extending up beyond the container's rim will allow the arranger to place each flower, leaf, and stem where she wishes it to remain. With such mechanics, stems can be placed in a deep container in a horizontal or vertical position.

When composing the arrangements, a large groundcloth is spread out and the plant material divided equally on it. Paired arrangements should be built simultaneously. Place a stem in one vase, a similar one in the other. Continue in this way until both compositions are complete. The arranger must have, of course, a preconceived idea of the silhouette the compositions will present and must stay within that boundary. The finished arrangement must not present a flat appearance but should be fully rounded in form. Keep in mind also that variations of fundamental three-dimensional forms are more interesting to the eye: an ellipsoid arrangement more than a strictly spherical one; a double pyramid more than one of equilateral sides.

In other places in the church buildings, a one-flower composition or an arrangement of fruit or vegetables may be just as beautiful as one containing many flowers. The main requisite for a single-flower arrangement is to select a beautiful specimen. Flower and foliage must be in an early stage of development and completely free of disease and blemish. Whenever possible, self-foliage and long stems should be included in the composition. Otherwise use foliage that is near the same texture as that of the flower. How the flower is placed in the container and against the background space will determine mood and motivation of the arrangement. For example, a single flower placed to "stare" into the face of the onlooker is never as intriguing as when placed to suggest action. A lily with lowered head may look demure, while one that faces skyward can give a feeling of aspiration. A nasturtium's spiraling stem or a poppy bud may carry a mischievous air.

The choice of flower and foliage will, of course, influence the size, type, form, color, and texture of the container you use. It must be harmonious with the background space in these respects and should be simple in form and undecorated in design. If a long stem is used with the flower and buds, a tall vase should be used. If no stem or a very short stem is used, the container should be flat or nearly so. This will allow the whole form of the flower to be shown to greatest advantage.

To return to general instructions in creating an arrangement, when you have placed the basic structural material, stand back and study your design. If you are using a Lazy Susan, turn it from side to side. Remember you are building a three-dimensional arrangement, and it must be complete from every side, regardless of how it is to be viewed. Design-test it with these questions:

1. Are the materials assembled for the arrangement in proper scale to each other and to the container and space they are to occupy?

2. Is the design right, in proportion to container and background space?

3. Are balance and counterbalance established?

4. Do the lines of the plant material follow the lines of the container?

5. Are spacings between stems pleasing and varied?

6. Are stems of unequal length (except when symmetrically planned)?

7. Is order in the design becoming apparent?

If you wish to superimpose contrasting flowers against structural lines to form interesting design, it is helpful to indicate general lines and forms by drawing them in the air with your hand, thus establishing certain boundaries as you proceed.

Now you may be ready for the point of emphasis, provided you feel one is needed. When constructing a line arrangement, a focal point of emphasis is not always required, for the convergence of lines toward a common center is often emphasis enough.

Your point of emphasis in other than a pure line arrangement may be an open-faced flower, a large single flower, a group of flowers, or one in contrasting color. Or it may be a carefully chosen figurine or woodform; a shell, rock, or other dominant feature. Place it at the median line where axes cross in a formal or symmetrical arrangement. In an asymmetrical one, it will be either to the right or to the left of center and where axis has been established.

Detailed material should be placed now. Larger plant material, usually rounded in form, is placed near the base of the container, and smaller flowers gradated in size upward in the arrangement. Transitional material may be called for—feathery, dainty plant forms for

FIG. 50. This long-lasting arrangement is notable for the strong contrast between the coppery toned juniper wood-form and its well-marked perpendicular grain with that of the fluffy sprays of warm beige Choris grass placed to follow the form of the wood. The large pyramidal quartz rock at its base, with its horizontal lines, adds to the strong masculine feeling of this composition. This type of arrangement is suitable for the out-door area of a church or for the men's meeting room.

filling in gaps and holes. (These are listed on page 186 as "fillers.") It is not necessary to use every single piece of material you have gathered for the composition. Avoid using too much foliage or too many different kinds of foliage in an arrangement. Broad leaves will often take away a fussy look. When you have feathery foliage, use simple forms in flowers and fruits. If flower forms seem "busy," choose broad leaves. Don't be afraid to vary heights and spacings, if necessary, to heighten interest in the arrangement. Ask yourself again:

1. Is the arrangement appropriate to time, place, occasion?

2. Is it proportionate to container and to setting?

3. Are the flowers and other plant material and accessories in proper scale with each other, with container, and setting also?

4. Is balance established by the placement of the first lines or forms? Are there balance and counterbalance in colors and sizes as well as forms?

5. Are the colors, values, textures, and shapes harmonious with each other, with container, and with setting?

6. Is there a feeling of rhythm, leading the eye through the arrangement?

7. Is there a dominant feature with other materials subordinate to it? Does subordinate material follow dominant forms and lines?

8. Are the colors in container and plant material blended by placing a mirror or a colored mat under glass, silver, or pewter container?

9. Is the transitional material used wisely in leading the eye from point to point and to the place of emphasis?

10. Does the arrangement as a whole hang together? Are the parts interrelated in such a way that each part is necessary to the whole?

11. Will plant material be kept from leaning on container or tabletop when the arrangement has been placed?

12. Are the associated values harmonious throughout?

13. If the plant material is long-lasting, will it be changed in some lines by movement in space, and perhaps deepened in color or solidity by long immersion? If so, will it be placed near light in such a way as to improve the arrangement by movement over a long period of time?

14. Have any lines that cross and form angles been trimmed out?

15. Has color-sandwiching—a deep color between light ones, or vice versa—been avoided?

16. Are lines going the same way to produce rhythm?

17. Do container and contained tie together in color at rim line?

18. Has plant material been brought down over edge, to break rim-line?

19. Has the original plan for the arrangement been achieved?

20. Is it well balanced and in good taste? Does it convey a feeling of movement, grace, and charm?

If the answers to these questions are mainly affirmative, your arrangement is good and you have achieved true artistry. (See Chapter 12 for decorating the High Altar.)

✍ 9 ✍

Evolving Ideas for Church Bazaars

Pictorial arrangements have a definite place in floral decoration for the church school or recreation rooms. They are often interesting in themselves and make delightful holiday pieces. There are two kinds of pictorial arrangements: figure and landscape.

Figure portraiture calls for a dominant object to be used. It may be a figurine of good design, a rhythmic piece of wood, a shell, a beautiful rock, fungi, or some other arresting natural object. Whatever is used becomes the center of interest and is treated as a portrait, so to speak—all accompanying plant material being subordinated to it. In this sort of arrangement, the concern is not to make the plant material look as if it were growing naturally; it is used only to produce an effect or to frame and enhance the central object of interest. It should be placed to follow the lines of the dominant feature, and should be harmonious in feeling, color, texture, and kept in scale. If a figurine is to be used, it must convey a feeling of life. It may be dynamic, but the pose or stance must never give the impression that the object is about to jump out of the scene. The choice of the figurine is all-important. If it represents a living being, consider how its living counterpart looks.

There are exquisite hand-carved wooden pieces that lend charm and interest to an arrangement, if the plant material used is in harmony and in scale with the figure. If more than one figurine is used, they should be grouped near the center of the composition, facing inward. Three is a good number (depending, of course, on the type of arrangement) but usually not more than five. The way the figures are placed against the background will add much to the distinction of the composition. To gain unity with the background, a standing figure or bust would do well against a vertical panel, and a reclining figure or perhaps a long, low-lying piece of wood placed horizontally would be best against a horizontal background.

The background space and general type of room will suggest the type of balance one should employ. If the background is formal and symmetrical, the figure should be placed in the exact center of the arrangement. The plant material should be manipulated as a frame around the figure and should also be symmetrical in design.

If the arrangement is to be asymmetrical, place figurines where the axis is established. Remember to keep lines simple and going the same way. Use few forms and repeat their contour. Keep the point of emphasis where axes cross. Cover pin frog or other mechanics of construction. Feel your way in this kind of arrangement by studying good paintings. Experiment. Use your imagination. Your creative instinct will lead you along new and exciting paths. Set your arrangements apart from other objects and frame them with backgrounds, such as screens, mirrors, niches, leaves, or other types of frames.

Naturalistic Landscapes

Here you simulate trees with twigs, grass with moss, boulders with pebbles, cliffs with rocks, lakes with mirrors. There is little left for the arranger to do except to assemble the materials that are alike in feeling so as to tell a story with them. Careful choice of figures holds as true in this as in portrait composition.

In a landscape design, the order of preference is reversed. Here the plant material is dominant and the figure or figures subordinate. Since all figurines have a tendency to steal the attention in a composition, this may be reduced in a landscape design by half hiding the creatures and by careful selection as to dullness of finish and harmony of texture. As stated elsewhere, dipping a figurine in soapy water or buttermilk will dull the finish.

Begin by establishing your preconceived idea of a landscape scene. You may start with the figurine, which can set the scale or relationship of sizes; but remember, it must not dominate. A rule of thumb: tree, ten times the height of a man. The basic principles applicable to all forms of visual art are followed: harmony, proportion, scale, texture, color, balance. Scale is the most important, as it sets the size relationship. Build your plant material around the figure, considering size, color, sense of rhythm. For instance, if the figure is small, choose grasses to simulate trees; if the figure has a wind-blown look, search for plant materials that give that same rhythmic feeling and repeat its lines. Make sure the light and dark foliage are used carefully, to avoid spotty effects and by using more of one value than the other. Place large leaves, mirrors, plaques, small screens to form an enclosure, because you are seeking to establish a feeling of reality in a landscape design and must keep it as a unit, where each element is in true scale.

In planning a snow scene, indentations and shadows may be suggested by scattering small amounts of dry soil or chalk dust. This will give a feeling of depth and solidity to objects used in the scene. In using rocks or "trees," the ones in the foreground should be larger and deeper in color, becoming lighter or grayer as they diminish in size in the background. As in all floral composition, the quality of a landscape design depends on scale and relatedness of objects, their appropriateness to one another, and proper perspective. Success with Lilliputian scenes may lead you to try landscapes on a larger scale. Start now and try your wings!

Miniature and Small Arrangements

The over-all size of a miniature arrangement is 6 inches, which includes container and stand, if used. This type of arrangement is satisfactory and can bring much pleasure if one enjoys working in small dimensions with small materials, and has patience and good vision. The same principles of design are involved as in a larger floral composition. Scale must be carefully considered in choice of materials and figurines in an arrangement of this size. A miniature arrangement should be set apart, because it is necessarily out of scale with other objects in a room. It may be placed in a recess or on a shelf in a frame, before a mirror, screen, large leaf, or fan.

Small arrangements usually measure an over-all size of 6 to 8 inches. They serve a wider range of purpose than do miniature ones, in that they are a better size to use on a tray or a bedside table, in a bathroom, dressing room, or child's room, or on a coffee table.

Plant material suitable for miniature and small arrangements may be found in the listings headed "Fillers," on page 186. These are dainty, fine materials such as grasses, weeds, and tiny flowers: violets, sweet William, phlox, coral-bells, forget-me-nots, alyssum.

Many household objects may be used as containers for such arrangements: thimbles, sample perfume bottles, hollow knobs. Buttons, jewelry, and other trinkets also may be used. Novelty shops show a good assortment of miniature objects made primarily for charm bracelets. Oriental shops are another good source of supply.

Long-lasting arrangements are of great convenience to the alert flower arranger who is interested in creating beauty at a minimum of time and expense and are a boon when fresh-cut materials are scarce and costly. From a contemporary viewpoint with respect to this, it is not implied that the new look has anything in common with the old look of very dead, very dry "decorations" that used to grace grandmother's front parlor. The blossoms, seedpods, grasses, and peacock feathers that were crammed into narrow-necked vases to compete with floral embellishment on the sides of the container have been banished. Beautiful earth-toned, open-throated containers of good design are used to advantage for arrangements of dried plant material, and whatever is used in a dried arrangement should be colorful and lovely in form.

Preserving Flowers

Fresh flowers may be treated for drying and preservation of form and color by the following procedure:

In a cardboard box place such dainty materials as pansies, columbine, primroses, daffodils, tulips, open-faced, completely fresh roses, Iceland, Oriental, Shirley poppies, etc., on a bed of vermiculite or peat moss, sand or borax, 2 inches deep, making sure no petals overlap. Place at least 3 more inches of bed material on top. Lay the box gently down and place uncovered in oven. The pilot light must be on, but no greater heat. Let stand in oven 4 to 10 days. Carefully remove material and gently brush away with cotton any bedding material that remains.

Our grandmothers used warm sand and powdered borax, but did not place flowers in an oven. The writer has had success with this method; materials are light and easy to handle. The theory behind this method is to draw the moisture from the plant material quickly but without damage to form or color of it. It is most important that the flowers be absolutely fresh before they are processed. The vermiculite is a good lightweight medium in which to store or transport delicate dried plant materials and delicate containers.

We have learned also that certain fresh flowers keep exceptionally well and are very satisfactory when combined with woodforms. They may be inserted into the arrangement in concealed pickle jars, and when they fade may be replenished with more fresh flowers or fruit, succulents, grasses, seedpods that also last well. Thus, variety may be gained without complete upheaval.

If woodforms are used, they may become the dominant material and the basic design of the arrangements. The placement of fresh materials should follow their general lines and be harmonious in color and texture. If succulents are added to such an arrangement, damp moss (sphagnum) may be placed beneath them and will keep them fresh, and after a time they will begin to grow. Succulents are especially harmonious with woods of various kinds. Try gray-green succulents with the copper tones of juniper roots.

The vegetable kingdom yields its share of interesting shapes, sizes, and colors for long-lasting arrangements. Try using such vegetables as gourds, strawberry and Indian corn, okra pods, seedpods. Vegetables are appropriate in arrangements for harvest festivals and similar parish social activities and are at home in either a traditional or contemporary setting.

Transporting Materials for Arrangement

Be ever on the alert for materials to collect for use in flower arrangements: gnarled branches, woodforms, moss, mistletoe, rocks, lichens, fungi, shells. Collect such flowers as cockscomb, statice, yarrow, everlasting, and any other strong-bodied flowers or leaves that keep their color and shape when dried.

The gathering of plant materials, their transportation and storage, are problems requiring careful preliminary thought. A ski rack on top of the car is a boon for transporting light, fragile materials, such as grasses and seedpods. Before starting on a trip, pack the ski rack with long cardboard cartons. In each one place tissue paper to wrap the materials when gathered. At the time of gathering, wrap them in tissue, and label each carton with the name of the materials, where found, date, and any other pertinent facts you may need later. Take along a plastic cover for the rack, to protect the cartons from dust and moisture. Wrap any rocks or heavy objects in newspapers and place them on the floor or in the lugguage compartment of the car.

Skeletonizing leaves is difficult; however, the results may be very satisfying. The strong-bodied varieties are best for this process— leaves like magnolia, laurel, ivy, avocado. The leaves must be boiled gently in soapy water, using yellow soap and adding 1 tablespoon of soda and 1 teaspoon of glycerin to each quart of water. The length of boiling time varies: not too much, not too little. The leaves are then lifted from the hot soapy water and tap water allowed to run gently over them. Eventually the outer case will give way and the chlorophyll will spill into the sink. If you are very careful, the entire exquisite skeleton of the leaf will be preserved. After the chlorophyll has been washed away, the leaves may be spread out to dry. They will stiffen and may then be glued to stems and placed among flowers and grasses in an arrangement, lending to it the utmost delicacy and laciness.

Photo Russell Illig   *Fern Bowers Hunt*

FIG. 51. Skeletonized magnolia leaves were wired to a wire frame to form this Christmas wreath. The frame was first wrapped with white ribbon to prevent the leaves from slipping. After the leaves were in place, and going the same way, a string of red bead ornaments was wound between each second leaf. Three red ornaments with a spray of camellia leaves were wired to the top of the frame to simulate fruit. This type of wreath should be hung in a window so as to show the delicate veining of the leaves.

Photo Russell Illig   *Fern Bowers Hunt*

FIG. 52. Algerian ivy leaves were skeletonized to make this lacelike tree. Each leaf was wired to a stiff one, and then placed in a heavy brass container to hold it upright. Sequins and tiny ornaments complement the jeweled star on top.

Simulated Fruit Tree (Popcorn Tree)

It is possible to evolve a blossoming fruit tree out of season. Choose a suitable branch or small tree and glue white jumbo popcorn on the buds along the stems. To obtain the best results, "adhesive bond" is applied generously to the back side of the kernels. Let stand until the bond becomes tacky, then stick the kernels to the nodes. As a backdrop simulating an orchard or a distant scene, a popcorn tree creates the illusion of April in January.

Evergreen Rope Garlands

Materials needed: Scissors, cotton rope, spool of pliable wire, dye.

Step 1: Cut 4-inch tips from long-keeping plant material. (Choose colors to harmonize with background and occasion.) Condition by submerging in water for 4 hours.

Step 2: Rope should have been dyed the color of the leaves.

Step 3: Take leaf tips from water, shade and wire to cotton rope that has been attached to some object at doorknob height. Hold rope in left hand and begin garland by overlapping each succeeding sprig and wire to rope. Work all around the rope until desired length is completed.

Suggestion: Interesting effects can be gained by using broad-leaf material together with the tips of the needle varieties, or by interspersing fruit, such as apples or cranberries, at regular intervals along rope.

Fruit and Leaf Combinations

The following combinations are suitable for Della Robbia garlands, swags, and wreaths. Select fruit and leaves that keep well and are suitable to the planned background as to size, color, and texture.

1. **White and green:** Ivy (white and green variegated) may be used with white snowberries and with fruits that have been slightly sprayed with magic snow.

2. **Yellow, orange, and green:** Yellow euonymus, golden privet, with yellow apples. Green persimmons, oranges, kumquats, tangerines, yellow apples, pittosporum fruits, and red-orange berries. Lady apples, green and red berries, lemons and limes, hawthorn apples, rose hips, bittersweet fruit pods are in colors that are lovely when used with brass. Choose olive or moss-green ribbon.

3. **Red, yellow, and green:** Green seeds from palm trees and *Arbutus unedo* fruits. Red pomegranates, red and yellow apples, lemons, green and yellow lady apples, green and red berries, red cranberries.

4. **Brown and green:** Brown magnolia leaves or glycerin-treated ones. Choose only chartreuse, green, and yellow fruits and berries, such as green apples, grapefruit, lemons, limes, green berries.

5. **Gray and rose:** Dollar eucalyptus, gray-green hen-and-chickens, pepper berries, seedpods of *Magnolia grandiflora*.

FIG. 53. This Della Robbia garland follows the architectural lines of the doorway. The dark green leaves of the English laurel in the garland are set off by the rich brown oak panels of the woodwork. The red apples accent the center of the garland and tie harmoniously to other Christmas decorations in the room.

Photo Esther Wagner   *Fern Bowers Hunt*

FIG. 54. Della Robbia garlands and swags made of English laurel and bright red apples add a festive note to this hallway fireplace during the Christmas holidays. Red apples and laurel leaves are also placed on the wrought iron candlesticks at either end of the mantel.

6. **Gray-green, purple, and violet:** Dollar eucalyptus, small egg-plants, kumquats, eugenia or raphiolepis, and Japanese privet berries. Fill in with rose-colored, everlasting dried flowers in shades of lavender and purple.

Della Robbia Wreath

Materials needed: 3 wire circles (each a different diameter) to form a cradle; 4-inch wide roll of wax paper, preferably green; florist pins (hairpin type); wire, 12 inches long, 20 gauge; fruits; broad leaves in colors harmonious with fruits; a sphagnum or tree moss.

Step 1: Prepare leaves in the same way as for garlands. Tightly pack wire cradle with damp moss.

Step 2: Wrap frame with wax paper. Slightly overlap each wrap and secure last lap in place with florist pin.

Step 3: Lay frame flat on table. Draw a circle 2 inches smaller than the smallest ring in cradle; this will help keep center of the wreath clean-cut and round, by working above the circle and bringing up the ends of the leaves to the inside circle mark.

Step 4: Begin to pin leaves to frame. Start at top and work around frame. Pin first one leaf on either side of frame, allowing each tip to just touch the table. Pin well back on each leaf. Pin a third leaf over the back half of the first two, allowing its tip end to just cover the pins of the first two. Place each succeeding leaf in the same manner. The two side leaves should barely overlap the midrib of the first two. Each third or top leaf should overlap about half its length. Continue pinning leaves in this manner around wreath. Pins should be completely covered, so it is wise to experiment in overlapping, to get the best results.

Step 5: When the frame is completely covered with leaves, pin carefully selected fruit to it (see page 120 for method). The fruit design may be in the form of a crescent, placed at intervals of equal distance, or packed solid on the frame. Keep in mind the principles of good design and always work outward from a dominant piece at center, graduating to smaller sizes at outer perimeter. Fill in holes with berries, small fruits, or the tip ends of long-keeping plants such as pittosporum.

Swags Using Fruit or Cones

Materials needed: Hardware cloth (rabbit wire); stapler, scissors; tin snips; ribbon 1 to 3 inches wide, depending on size of swag; wire,

Photo Esther Wagner   *Fern Bowers Hunt*

FIG. 55. Spruce cones and magnolia leaves are formed into a door swag. The leaves have been glycerined and have taken on a deep, rich brown appearance. These are stapled to a paper pattern, which is in turn fastened to hardware cloth. The cones are then wired through the paper to the wire cloth. Green and brown two-toned ribbon is placed to cascade from the cone arrangement.

FIG. 56. This mantel decoration of cones and pine boughs is suitable for home, church, or recreation room during the holidays. Each cone is drilled at its base and wire is inserted. This is in turn wired to nails placed on a board the size of the mantel. Before the decorations are placed, the mantel is covered with green paper.

12 inches long, gauges, 18 and 22; buckram; friction tape; paper for pattern; fruits; leaves (glycerined).

Step 1: Pre-care of plant material as in simple garlands.

Step 2: Cut leaves from branches, place in 3 piles—small, medium, large.

Step 3: Measure background space.

Step 4: Make paper pattern for swag.

Step 5: Lay paper pattern over piece of stiff buckram and cut pattern.

Step 6: Staple broad leaves to buckram. Place first row close together around outer edge. These should extend over edge of buckram about 1 inch. Each succeeding row of leaves should overlap the one below and should be stepped back toward center like shingles. Make sure each staple is covered by a leaf.

Step 7: Cut hardware cloth with tin snips to fit buckram pattern. Bind raw edges with friction tape.

Step 8: Wire hardware cloth to the back of leaf-covered buckram shape.

Step 9: Wire fruit of choice to buckram- and leaf-covered shape.

Fruit Design. Group fruit as to color and size. Thread No. 18 gauge wire through stem end of each piece and fasten to frame. Begin with a dominant form, such as a pomegranate or apple in the center. Work outward toward perimeter with smaller-size fruit in harmonious colors, such as lemons, limes, lady apples. Fill in spaces with berries and small fruits, such as cranberries or hawthorn apples, or with tip ends of leafy twigs of long-lasting material. The entire pattern need not be covered with fruit, but allow some leaves to show. Experiment to get desired effect. If fruit design is arranged in crescent form, ribbon bows with streamers, or small bunches of fruit, may be attached at points of crescent. Cones may be used instead of fruit.

Glycerined Leaves

Make a new cut on freshly cut graceful branches of any strong-bodied, broad-leafed tree, including deciduous varieties. If the latter are used, they should be selected before autumn and before they are ready to fall.

Solution: 1 part glycerin to 2 parts water.

Place stem ends in the above solution, adding more in this proportion as the leaves begin to take it up. Allow branches to remain in solution 3 to 6 weeks in a cool room. Leaves will turn very dark if

left too long. Watch for choice color, then remove. Leaves most satis
factory to glycerin are copper beech, laurel, magnolia, redbud, eucalyptus.

Long-lasting arrangements can be made for use in the church with
graceful branches of glycerin-treated leaves. They should be placed in
vases without water. If flowers are combined with them, these can be
put into water-filled, small pickle jars and the jar concealed within the
larger container. Thus the flowers can be replaced from time to time
without disturbing the leaves. Flowers that have been dried with the
leaves and that have retained their color may also be used, such as
strawflower, yarrow, celosia, Chinese lantern, hydrangea.

❧ 10 ❧

Floral Arrangements for Personal Adornment in Weddings

She maketh a garland that is veray shene
wyth true-loves wrought in many a coloure
Replete with sweetnes and dulcet odoure.

It seems quite fitting that a chapter in a book on floral decoration for churches be devoted to flower arrangements made specifically to be worn or carried. Brides' and bridesmaids' bouquets, corsages, boutonnieres, leis—all these might fall within the range of creativity of an arranger who works frequently in connection with church life. The same basic principles of good design apply to the making of these as to any other thoughtfully executed arrangement. Consideration should be given to occasion, season, time of day, and harmony of components; in the case of a bouquet to be carried or a particular corsage to be worn by an individual, it should be scaled to the correct size for the recipient. These types of arrangements call forth real creative talent. Well made and cared for, they will last through a day and in many instances will keep for several days. Only flowers of good keeping quality should be used, and they must be absolutely fresh and free of blemish. When a corsage is not being worn, it should be placed on a damp cotton pad in a cellophane box or envelope and stored in the vegetable crisper box of a refrigerator or other cool place. A corsage is worn pinned to the shoulder or fastened to a velvet wristband. A recent vogue is to wear arrangements of tiny flowers as earbobs, and flowers are sometimes worn in the hair in lieu of a hat.

A cluster of corsages massed in the center of a table, each tied with a ribbon streamer leading to an individual place setting, is an interesting way to provide table decoration for a luncheon. Trays of boutonnieres or corsages are an attractive source of revenue at a church bazaar, or to give a fillip of added enjoyment to a particularly festive church social gathering.

Materials Needed

It is a wise and economical measure to provide a roomy box or basket in a convenient place to hold impedimenta for corsage-making. Special materials other than those listed on page 161 for a floral workshop include:

1. Six bundles of wire in 1-foot lengths, gauges 20, 22, 26, 28, 32, 34. Size 20 is heavy and size 34 is fine. Sizes 22 and 28 are perhaps the only sizes needed by the amateur.

2. Six tennis-ball cans or water glasses to hold wire.

3. Wire cutter.

4. Sharp scissors.

5. Sharp pocketknife for cutting stems.

6. Floratape or Parafilm for wrapping stems. These come in a variety of colors—greens, white, and brown. Floratape should be kept wrapped in wax paper and stored in a cool place.

7. Ribbon for bows, in material that does not spot and in a variety of colors and widths.

8. Cellophane or paper shields or strong-bodied leaves. These are used to fit around heads of flowers with a weak calyx, and also to

---

Fig. 57. Methods of wiring corsages.

(*Left, top*) **No. 1.** Daffodils and China lilies are used together to make this gay spring corsage. Gray-green bow matches the daffodil and China lily stems. The stems are grouped together, wrapped, and tied.

(*Right, top*) **No. 2.** White chrysanthemums encircle a red rosebud. A lace doily is slipped up around the stems and a crisp white bow is placed around covered stem. This may be carried by a young girl at a wedding.

(*Left, center*) **No. 3.** White carnations surround blue violas in a pleasing nosegay type of corsage. A crisp white ribbon bow holds a lace doily in place. Clutch method.

(*Right, center*) **No. 4.** A white rose is flanked by white stephanotis florets. The single piercing method is used here on the rose and the clutch method on the stephanotis. Olive-green, nonspot ribbon was used for a bow.

(*Bottom*) **No. 5.** White chrysanthemums, double hairpin method. Instead of ribbon, gray-green strap leaves of the iris are used to make a bow for the corsage.

protect clothing. They also provide a stable structure to pin to and wire through when using flowers that have a tendency to shatter.

9. Box of cotton tabs.

10. Cellophane boxes or bags in which to store corsages when they are not being worn.

11. Syringe to spray flowers.

12. Cellophane or paper doilies in a variety of sizes for French-type corsage.

13. Cellophane tape for securing petals.

14. Elastic bands to hold bunches of tiny flowers, such as pansies, violets, forget-me-nots, violas.

15. Corsage pins in a variety of colors.

16. Paraffin wax to drop in centers of some flowers to keep them from "going to sleep."

Gather plant material several hours before the flowers are to be used. Follow instructions for pre-care and hardening, just as for any floral arrangement.

1. Assemble all equipment on worktable and place flowers and leaves on tray covered with damp cotton. Cut stems to 1-inch stubs.

2. Sit with light falling over left shoulder or at back; never work under fluorescent light because flower colors will be distorted. Use daylight-corrected light globes.

3. Experiment with second-class blooms before trying to make a corsage with the more choice ones. The techniques of wiring and taping flowers are the most important steps to learn in corsage-making. When these are mastered, you can advance to the more complex construction of a bride's bouquet.

Wiring (see p. 128)

Wiring provides artificial, flexible stems. It reduces bulkiness, secures and strengthens heavy-headed flowers, and allows for latitude in the design of a corsage. One may curve a wired stem and it stays in place.

1. **Single-piercing** is the easiest method for a novice to follow in learning to wire a corsage. It is accomplished by introducing one wire through a strong calyx, such as a rose's, carnation's or daffodil's. (Other flowers having a strong calyx are listed on page 197.) The flower is held in the left hand (with damp fingers), blossom head down. Thread a No. 22-gauge wire through the calyx. Draw it through halfway. Bend

ends of wire down to form stem and tape them together to form a single stem.

2. **Double-piercing** is a method accomplished the same way as single-piercing, except that two wires are used instead of one. Such heavy-headed flowers as tuberous begonia, camellia, gardenia have a tendency to shatter and need support by two wires. This sort of flower may be further strengthened by placing two or more strong-bodied leaves, such as ivy, laurel, or camellia around the calyx. The wires are threaded through leaf and calyx in such a way as to catch the leaf on the opposite side. The flower head is then turned halfway and another wire introduced. For instance, the two wires are pierced through the calyx at right angles and equidistant from each other. Three wires are then bent down to form a stem. A fourth wire is wrapped around the three to secure them in place. They are now ready to be taped.

3. **The hook method** is used when small flowers and florets, such as those of hyacinth and stephanotis, are wired or taped separately to be grouped with larger flowers in a corsage. Insert a No. 28 wire down through each tiny flower or floret. Bend a ¼-inch or less hook at one end of the wire and pull the hook down through flower to make stem, and tape. Bell-shaped flowers lend themselves to this method.

4. **The hairpin method** is used for leaves and flowers like chrysanthemum and daisy. Bend a 24-gauge wire into a hairpin shape. Insert the two ends through center of each flower, pull down to form a stem, and tape. Use this method also for wiring leaves, straddling the mid-rib of the leaf with a 28-gauge wire bent like a hairpin, and tape.

5. **The splint method** is used for such delicate and dainty flowers as the orchid, lily, and rhododendron. A piece of wet cotton is wrapped around the base of the flower or floret. The flower is held in the left hand and a piece of 22-gauge wire 12 inches long is wrapped twice around the cotton-wrapped base. The loop is made in the middle of the wire so as to leave the two ends free. Bend one wire down to form a stem and wire the other end around the base and stem of flower. The second wire is then bent down to strengthen the wire stem. In this type of wiring, no wire pierces the flowers. Care must be taken that the wire does not cut into the flower, but the clutch wire must be tight enough to prevent the flower from slipping from this improvised splint.

Taping provides a smooth covering for stems, conserves the moisture in the flowers, and protects clothing from stains and moisture. It is easily mastered and makes an attractive finish to a corsage. Hold the flower head gently in the left hand, the tape in the right hand. Begin to wrap well up on the calyx of a flower (above where it has been wired). Stretch the end of the tape and secure it in place around the calyx. Wrap the tape around the calyx a couple of times, pinching as you wrap. With flower in left hand, tape in right, start to twirl flower, holding tape still and at an angle. Twirl stem until it is entirely covered; then tear off tape—never cut it. Smooth stem up and down with fingers to give it a neat appearance.

After flowers, florets, and leaves have been wired and taped, assemble them according to the plan you have in mind. Group buds at outer perimeter, larger flowers in center. Keep in mind color and texture harmony. Secure the assembled stems by wrapping them with 28-gauge wire. Cover exposed wire with tape. The corsage is now ready for the ribbon bow.

Bows are a charming addition to a corsage and may be the means of tying colors and textures of flowers to costume. They should be made with care, and a bow should never be more prominent than the flowers. Choose ribbon of good quality that is nonspotting. Keep bow harmonious in color and texture with stems and leaves rather than with flowers. Strap leaves such as Dutch iris or narcissus may be made into bows for corsages. These are appropriate for daytime wear.

To make a bow, loop ribbon between forefinger and thumb of left hand. As you catch the loop with little finger of left hand, give it a half-twist with the right hand. Pinch it with thumb and forefinger so as to keep satin side of ribbon facing out. Make four or five loops. Grasp loops in the exact middle and secure with a bobby pin. This leaves the hands free to cut an 8-inch piece of ribbon. Twist this piece 4 or 5 times in the exact middle and tie it around center of loops. Remove bobby pin. Tie bow to corsage. Bows may also be made of lace, velvet, metallic braid, or cord.

French Bouquets

Split the calyx of a carnation, remove seed head from center of flower and insert a tiny rosebud which has been surrounded with forget-me-nots. Forget-me-nots should first be arranged in small bunches, their stem ends wrapped with wet cotton, wired, and taped. After this, they are placed around the rosebud and securely wrapped with a fine wire. This compact mass is placed in the exact center of the carnation, and it, in turn, is wrapped with tape. A hole is cut in the center of a cellophane doily. This is slipped up and around the stems to form a frill for the corsage. A ribbon bow in a harmonious color is added under the frill. This nosegay may be used on a package, carried by a very young person, or placed with other similar bouquets to decorate a table.

One can experiment with many kinds of plant material and evolve interesting and original designs for personal adornment. At Christmas time seedpods, tiny cones, and hard candies may be wrapped and incorporated into the design of a corsage.

It is important to remember that a corsage must not appear too heavy, that stems come from a common center, and that simplicity is always the essence of good taste and often a measuring rod for beauty.

Your preconceived idea for floral decoration, whether it is for a small corsage or for a huge *fiesta,* must be worked out to your complete satisfaction and must give aesthetic pleasure to the beholder if it is to be considered worthy of this art.

Leis

The vogue of wearing leis for weddings and other occasions is currently in high favor throughout the United States. This charming practice came to us from Hawaii and other islands of the Pacific. There, leis are worn by both men and women for any and all occasions, regardless of time of day or season of year. For the uninitiated, a lei may be explained as a garland of flower heads or other plant material strung bead-fashion on a stout string. Leis are usually worn as necklaces but may be used as armlets, wristlets, or crowns. They are appropriate for a bride and her attendants, and are popular for any festivity where a bouquet might be carried or a corsage worn. In the Pacific islands, incoming travelers are welcomed with leis, and they are used often as traveling gifts.

The use of leis is not confined to personal adornment, however. They are used to festoon church social rooms and public buildings on many an occasion. For a gala reception, mantels, doorways, and pictures may be hung with leis, where flowers are plentiful. At Christmas, street lamps are hung with leis; in churches, pulpits, candelabra, and pillars lend themselves beautifully to this type of decoration. Leis make unusual and striking decorations for Christmas trees.

Choosing Material for Leis. Leis are simple and fun to make. Since a lei must contain a great number of individual flowers and leaves, it follows that one should be assured of an ample supply. For example, a lei 42 inches long will contain approximately 60 flower heads the size of a carnation. A lei made of smaller flowers, such as bachelor button or Vanda orchid, will require more than 150 flower heads. Also, when the smaller flowers are used in a lei, more than one strand is usually worn. The material chosen for a lei will depend on many factors: availability, occasion, season, and the person for whom or place for which it is intended. A bride might choose a lei of tuberoses in place of the conventional wedding bouquet or one of baby wood-roses or seedpods to wear with a tweed going-away suit.

Only strong-bodied, preferably fragrant flowers that keep well should be used in leis. Among the most satisfactory for springtime are daffodils, hyacinths, tulips, Siberian iris, crocus, forsythia, freesias, and violets. Corsican hellebore blossoms, where available, also make beautiful leis. Among summer flowers adaptable to this form of decoration are carnations, pinks, strawflowers, bachelor button, gladiolus, cosmos, and rosebuds. In California or other places having a similar climate, agave florets, gloriosa lilies, tuberoses, francoa, Mexican poppies, agapanthus, hibiscus, day lilies, and tuberous begonias make beautiful leis. Autumn provides Michaelmas daisies, chrysanthemums, marguerites, asters, and strawflowers.

Dried flowers, such as strawflowers, baby woodroses, as well as eucalyptus pods, bittersweet, seedpods, and small cones, may be found in many places for use in winter leis. Also, in warm climates there are camellias and gardenias for winter bloom. Strong-bodied and colorful leaves may be used to good effect. Exotic flowers from the tropics and from greenhouses everywhere may be had at surprisingly moderate cost. Present-day rapid transporation and refrigeration make it possible for these to arrive at the florist's in excellent condition. Among the most popular are plumeria, ginger, picaca, poinciana, mauna loa, cape jasmine, stephanotis, bouvardia, and hibiscus. Orchids in variety, gardenias, crown flowers, and carnations are readily obtainable.

Step-by-Step Procedure. Condition all stems or leaves in deep water before using in leis. Cut flowers in early morning or late evening, choosing those just coming into bloom. Plunge stems in deep, cool water to their necks. Corsican hellebore, hydrangeas, violets, and leaves should be completely submerged. Add commercial preservatives to the water and place in cold, dark place to "harden" for 2 to 6 hours or more.

Remove pollen from lilies to prolong life and prevent staining petals and clothing. With a syringe, spray such flowers as camellias, hibiscus, and tuberous begonias, also cape jasmine and gardenias. When ready to make the lei, remove each flower from deep water and snip off its stem. Place it on a tray covered with damp cotton. Handle the flowers as little as possible and work with wet fingers to avoid bruising the petals. Where the calyx is of a bulky type, such as the carnation, snip it off. However, the calyx is often attractive when used in a lei and should be left on flowers wherever possible, to prevent shattering.

If you do not have a long, slender needle, make one out of piano wire by folding it over to make the eye and filing the opposite end to make the point. Or use a long, slender upholstery needle. Thread with nylon thread the same color as the flowers you intend to use. Make it the length needed. Pierce the needle through the calyx of the flower (if the calyx has been retained) or through the center of the flower. Push this first flower to the end of the needle. Add flowers until the needle is full, and then push on to the thread. Your method of threading flowers will determine the design and interest. You will want to experiment to get the desired effect. Keep in mind the principles of design and graduate the flowers in size and intensity of color. The larger flowers and deeper shades, for the sake of emphasis, should go toward the center of the lei.

The completed lei should give a round, full appearance, rather like an old-fashioned ruff or feather boa. When you are sure the lei is long enough and full enough, tie the ends of the thread together with a square knot. Then tie again. A lei may be worn more than once, provided it is made of long-keeping flowers and is returned to a covered tray in a cool place when not in use. Should your lei look "tired," immerse it for a second in hot water and then in cold water. Dampen the cotton on the tray and place tray and lei in a cool place.

Leaf Leis. Instead of stringing leaves on thread, staple them to a narrow, double-faced satin ribbon. Overlap each leaf, starting at one end of the ribbon, as though you were placing shingles on a roof. The staple is then hidden by the addition of the next leaf. For interesting effects use leaves of different shapes, colors, and sizes.

Seed and Pod Leis. The easiest way to make leis of seeds or pods is to string them while they are still fresh. Allow them to dry afterward, in a warm, airy place, already strung. If the pods and seeds are already dry when you work with them, holes can be bored in them with a small drill. An upholstery needle is excellent for stringing pods. Experiment with different forms, colors, and textures in seeds and pods. The variety is limitless.

FIG. 58. An all-white wedding bouquet composed at the center with Eucharist lilies. Cascading down from them are stephanotis and fragrant tuberoses. The lilies are encircled with a pleated frill of fine lace.

Fern Bowers Hunt

Wedding Bouquets

The same procedure is followed in the construction of a wedding bouquet as in making a formal corsage, with the exception that the wire stems for a wedding bouquet should be 6 to 8 inches long. After florets have all been wired and taped, group them together in the left hand, the larger flowers in the center, graduating outward to smaller ones. Each stem should vary in length, the smaller the flower, the longer the stem. Secure the stems together with a wire. Cover it with tape, then cover again with ribbon. Bend to form handle. Slip a collar up over handle and well up around the back of the bouquet. The collar may be encircled with a frill of fine lace, pleated ribbon, or left plain. Tip each wired floret to face forward.

Shower or Cascade Bouquets

Continue as above for a shower or cascade wedding bouquet, but attach varying lengths of double-faced satin ribbon streamers, ¼-inch wide, to back of bouquet before collar is placed. The longest streamer should not reach below the bride's knee, calculating from the waistline. Allow an extra ¼ yard of ribbon on each streamer for knots.

These should be placed equidistant every third of the length of each streamer. The knots will help hide the stem ends of florets which are attached to each streamer. Use only small flowers for this cascade effect. (See page 188 in Appendix for list of flowers suitable for formal and informal weddings.)

✌ 11 ✌

Suggestions for Teaching Children
Church Decoration

Go forth, under the open sky, and list
To Nature's teachings.

Most children respond readily and with enthusiasm to wise guidance in creating simple floral arrangements. The informal suggestions set forth here have proved helpful to church school teachers and to junior museum instructors, as well as to mothers wanting to share an aesthetic experience on a plane where the two generations can meet.

Teach children to show reverence and see beauty. Children can be taught reverence for their church and, more particularly, for the altar, if they are allowed to decorate their church school rooms; but first make them aware of beauty in the forms, colors, and textures of living things—in grasses, flowers, fruits, trees, hummingbirds, pebbles, shells. Their perception of the changing face of nature and her calendar of seasons can be heightened, and they can be made more sensitive to beauty. Ask each child to bring in some plant material that he thinks is beautiful. Guide each one into selecting simple forms, soft colors, and help each one to place the material in ordered form, but do not rigidly restrict a child's free expression of taste.

Teach children to feel beauty. Explore the fascinating field of textures. Perhaps in the autumn when classes have just begun and leaves are falling, you might have a lesson on leaves. Encourage the collection of many leaves so as to provide a variety of textures. Some will be woolly or smooth, harsh and rough, or satiny. Some will be prickly.

138

Point out the varieties of sizes and shapes—large or small; elongated or broad; round or squarish; and emphasize their veining and ordered form. Show them skeletonized leaves.

Teach children to understand and use plant material. Show the group how leaves may be combined in an arrangement. Place their own arrangements against different-colored backgrounds of soft but plain color. Discuss form, size, texture in flowers and plants. But do not as yet talk about color.

Ask the children to bring in small containers and berries or small flowers to be placed in them. Show the relationship of sizes by supplying extra materials that would be appropriate for each selection brought. Encourage the use of natural containers: shells, pieces of bark or wood, sturdy leaves, rocks. Point out how harsh glazes and gaudy colors in containers detract from the beauty of flowers and leaves.

Explain how mechanics of flower arrangement differ and what type is the most effective for use in certain arrangements. You will need:

Pin holders	Oil base clay
Chicken wire	Blunt scissors
Hardware cloth	Twistems
Sand	Pipe cleaners

Teach children to appreciate and conserve wayside growth. Explain conservation in home and church gardens. Explain why wayside growth should not be uprooted. Explain how the conservation of road-side weeds and grasses hold the soil and prevent erosion. Encourage the children to pick no more material than needed at a time. Place immediately in water in a cool place. Teach them about long-keeping plants—marguerites, daisies, chrysanthemums, succulents.

Call flowers by botanical names, giving the common names also but explaining that botanical names are common to every nation and language. Fix botanical names by telling stories about various plants. Have a lesson on plant symbolism (see Appendix, page 164). A short list of reference books suitable for teaching children may be found on page 212, but this should be supplemented from your own library and from your own knowledge of local plant life in your immediate neighborhood.

Color. Bring a prism to class. Show each child how a spectral band is formed when sunlight shines through a prism onto white paper. Ask each child to remember the various colors and to bring a sample of one hue in a flower or leaf for the next lesson. The teacher should provide several large ring molds and a number of smaller jello ring molds.

Choose, from among material brought in, flowers approximating spectrum colors. Again hold the prism up to the sunlight. Explain in a few words a parallel between the ring molds and a clockface. Now place a yellow flower at 12, a red-orange flower clockwise at 2, a magenta red at 4, a blue-violet at 6, a blue flower at 8, and a green leaf at 10. Go back and fill in intermediate colors that lie between, approximating them to color of wheel choice.

Design. The creation of floral arrangements is an excellent way to teach children the principles of good design. This should be done in a simple, direct manner, avoiding complicated patterns and ideas. Through this medium children will learn proportion, scale, balance, color, and value. By learning to create little Bible scenes with figurines they may be led to hobby interests, such as collecting rocks, making and decorating simple figurines, collecting shells or woodforms. Handling plant material and its arrangements may be a means whereby a child can acquire a sense of achievement. Creation of something well done is necessary to the mental and emotional development of every child.

Allow the children to help you plan a simple floral decoration for the altar or a table, one that is harmonious in color, texture, and feeling. Let them help plan a decoration around a holiday theme, provide food and napkins in keeping with the decoration, and have a party! The children will quickly grasp the idea that there is an aesthetic relationship between food and how it is presented.

Assemble materials for them. Allow children to bring small figurines of animals or beings to class. Encourage them to gather rocks, pebbles, driftwood, branches to simulate trees, etc. Perhaps a simple landscape scene could be constructed as a group project. Show harmony of proportion and scale in relation to materials used. For a flower arrangement and for landscapes, too, show how to place mechanics for correct construction: a dry container; warm clay on pin frog; a half-turn to secure.

Mass Arrangement. Show construction for a mass arrangement (pin frog plus daisy holder). Plan a one-color arrangement with leaves.

Line Arrangement. Children may be guided in making simple line arrangements with twigs. The same principles of composition apply as in advanced work, but should be stated simply and clearly, and not too much given in any one lesson. The chief concern should be clearness, so as not to confuse the child with complicated arrangements.

Fruits are easy to arrange. The teacher may supply a selection of bananas, oranges, grapefruit, and grapes, and after an arrangement is

Photo Esther Wagner   *Fern Bowers Hunt*

FIG. 59. An antique Mexican hand-carved wooden figure of the Madonna and Baby is surrounded by pine boughs and cones. The arrangement is placed in a window niche, where a votive candle burns in front of the figure during the holidays.

Fig. 60. How to make a few flowers look like many on Valentine's Day is achieved by using the broad leaves of the saxifrage, their blossoms, and a few carnations in three glass containers. A gold paper fan increases the size of the composition and ties the units together.

142

completed, divide it and let the children enjoy it. Explain that fruit arrangements for one meal should probably be eaten at the next. Here is a lesson in reverse (function follows form!). Explain that fruits should not be washed before being placed in an arrangement, but before being eaten they must be carefully washed.

OUTLINE FOR TEACHING AND LECTURING ON FLORAL DECORATION

I. *Objectives*

1. To help students and children to see and appreciate beauty in nature.
    a. Arrange field trips
    b. Arrange exhibits of collected materials
    c. Arrange materials harmoniously to suit containers and suitable backgrounds (mirrors, niches, wall panels)
    d. Show slides, moving pictures, scrapbooks
2. To teach unobtrusively fundamental principles
    a. Demonstrate these principles in arrangements
    b. Evaluate your own and student-composed arrangements
    c. Consider age level and environment of students or children
    d. Avoid using word "criticize" and substitute "evaluate"
    e. While demonstrating, never turn your back on your audience, as you will lose contact with them; invariably they will start to whisper
    f. Never pass material out when you are trying to keep group attention
    g. Evaluate each principle of design demonstrated
    h. Have each student keep a notebook
    i. Have students (especially children) cut flower illustrations from seed catalogs to harmonize with backgrounds and from furniture and home decoration magazines when flowers are not available. Encourage them to find colored ones
    j. Remember students will be more interested in arrangements that affect their daily activities: self-adornment, corsages, headbands, wristbands, arrangements for parties, etc.

k. Begin by showing students how to arrange a party for Halloween

l. Continue through seasons; have students suggest items for holiday party, listing material accordingly:
Thanksgiving
Christmas
New Year's Day
Lincoln's Birthday
St. Valentine's Day
St. Patrick's Day
April Fool's Day
May Day
June (graduation, showers, luncheons, weddings)
Fourth of July (planned in June)
Summer (suggestions for student collections: dried plant material, weeds, grasses, fungi, driftwood, rocks, shells, woodforms)
Fall—gather leaves, press, skeletonize, and dry flowers. Plan landscape scenes and figure portraiture, backgrounds and vistas

m. If teaching or lecturing a church-centered group, a course might be worked out to follow decoration according to church calendar

II. *Significant Aspects of Floral Composition*

1. Opportunity to learn basic principles of the art of floral composition, which are linked to those of painting and sculpture
2. Opportunity to realize the creative urge to artistic and emotional self-expression
3. Advantages of working in a living medium

III. *Methods of Accomplishment*

1. Consideration of type of church and furnishings
   a. Traditional, formal
   b. Contemporary, informal
   c. Hybrid—blend of designs
2. Rules express general principles; arranger should not feel slavishly bound to rigid adherence
3. Consideration of place arrangement planned for:
   a. Background color (walls) and what to use (see lists)

   b. Background space

   c. Altar or other part of church

   d. Special occasion or simply for daily enjoyment

  4. General principles of composition and design

IV. *Selection of Plant Materials*

  1. Flowers

  2. Trees

  3. Shrubs

  4. Grasses, rushes, sedges, reeds

  5. Figurine portraiture, scenes

  6. Fruits

  7. Collecting materials (see also under Containers and Accessories)

   a. Short-lived or long-lasting

   b. Planning for source material (succession of color, form, type)

   c. Cutting stage

V. *Containers and Accessories*

  1. Types (sketches)

  2. What to look for in choosing

   a. Simple form, unembellished

   b. Neutral tones

   c. Wide-throated, outflaring, without bulging sides and narrow neck

  3. Materials, manmade and natural

   a. Metal, glass, ceramic; natural (driftwood, shells, etc.)

   b. Some unusual ones: miner's pans, scales, etc.

  4. Accessories

   a. Importance of using only very good ones

   b. Consideration of relationship to whole arrangement

   c. Dominance (scale) versus subordination and why one or the other

  5. Background modifications

   a. Mirrors, plaques, bases, mats, screens, fabrics

   b. "Framing" an arrangement

  6. The fun of collecting

   a. Shared activity with family and friends

   b. Possible leading in to lifetime work or hobby

VI. *Working Procedure*

1. Assembling material and its pre-care
2. Consideration of where arrangement is to be placed (altar, chancel, social rooms, church school)
3. If special occasion, what prevailing atmosphere (weekly church service, special service, wedding, christening, holiday, social function, etc.)
4. Choice of container (close relation to what it will contain)
   a. Proportion to surroundings
   b. Harmony with plant material in color, form, texture

VII. *Evolving Ideas*

1. Skeletonized leaves
2. Simulated flowering branch
3. Preservation of delicate flowers by drying process
4. Long-lasting arrangements

VIII. *Visual Aids*

1. Motion pictures
2. Slides
3. Displays of specimen plants
4. Scrapbooks
5. Demonstrations
6. Line drawings on blackboard

❧ 12 ❧

Adorning the High Altar for Feast Days and Special Occasions

As Christianity spread westward from Rome, and worshipers were encouraged by the clergy to add floral decoration to their churches, it became necessary to lay down certain ecclesiastical directives to govern the placement of floral arrangements in the church and, more especially, on the altar. These rules designate when and where flowers may be placed, but they do not indicate what flowers shall be used nor what their colors shall be. Since the beauty inherent in most flowers, as well as their symbolic connotation, form a direct link in the worship, it follows that they should be chosen, as far as possible, to reflect the liturgical meaning of the office of the day, to express the spirit of great festivals and other occasions. To accomplish a unified and harmonious whole, the arranger should know just how the altar is dressed for various occasions, and be familiar with the symbolic meaning of each object placed on it. As a quick reference aid, a liturgical calendar is provided in Appendix VIII, page 203.

Altar

The High Altar (the most important altar in the church) is a sacred, immovable stone table on which the Eucharistic Sacrifice is celebrated. The altar must be elevated. It must be consecrated by a bishop. The altar symbolically signifies Christ and should be treated with utmost reverence. Care must be exercised by the arranger in decorating it, that it not be profaned by careless acts, such as dropping a heavy object on it or by marring it in any way.

147

The top of the altar (mensa) should be covered with four cloths. The first is a cerecloth waxed with sacred chrism (oil mixed with balsam and blessed) to protect the other linen cloths from moisture that might collect from the stone. Over the cerecloth are placed two clean white cloths which just cover the top of the altar. A third, the fair linen, covers the mensa and hangs down on either side nearly to the floor. All these cloths are blessed.

The front of the altar should be covered with a frontal (antependium, pallium altares). There should be one frontal for each color of the various liturgical seasons. These should be made of silk, brocade, velvet, or other fine material. They may be embroidered with suitable emblems of the office of the day. The frontal cloth is not blessed.

Flowers

The arranger of flowers for the church should bear in mind that the altar is a hallowed sacrificial table that should be attended by the respectful. To take part in the decoration of it is to render service equal in significance and worthiness to any other performed by a layman, and the spirit of that service should be one of humility, sincerity, and reverence.

Altar guild members should have a special sense of responsibility and devotion and should be chosen for these qualities. The duties and privileges of altar guild membership should not, above all, be thought of as merely social activity. The chairman of the altar guild, or an individual arranger, should consult with the pastor whenever possible in planning floral decoration for the altar and sanctuary, that every aspect of it may be harmonious with the coming service.

The liturgical directives allow field and garden flowers to be used, as well as commercially grown ones. Potted plants and artificial blooms also may be used. These latter must be expertly made of fine quality material, such as silk or cloth of gold or silver; they should be faithful imitations of the real thing, but regardless of their beauty, are never to be preferred over fresh flowers. Flowers may be used on festival days and in accordance with the feast being celebrated. Ecclesiastical directives do not allow flowers on the altar when the frontal is black or violet (see Liturgical Calendar, Appendix VIII, page 203).

Flowers should not be placed on the mensa, because neither flowers nor vases pertain directly to the Holy Eucharist. When they are per-

Fern Bowers Hunt

High Altar, Saint Anthony Catholic Church, Redwood City, Calif.

missible, the vases may be placed on a retable (gradin) back of the altar (C.E.I, XII, 12, 14). Restraint should govern the number of vases used; two to four are considered adequate. When a special day, such as Christmas, Easter, or a wedding occasion calls for more, they may be placed at either end of the altar on flower standards, also elsewhere in the chancel and sanctuary. The vases may be placed to flank the cross or the candlesticks; or, if more than two vases are used on the retable, they may alternate in placement with the candlesticks. Flowers may not be placed in front of the cross, nor should they extend in height beyond the transverse arm of the cross, nor in any way overshadow it. A flower arrangement must not be placed before the Tabernacle door nor above nor within it (cf. S.R.C. 2067[10], 2613[6], 2740[1]). Neither may an arrangement hide nor interfere with other adornments on the altar. Flowers should not be placed at the corners of the altar, or too close to the lighted candles; nor should an arrangement interfere with the lighting of the candles by the acolytes.

Flowers may not be placed on the chancel steps nor on the chancel rail nor at any place where they might interfere with the actions of the clergy.

Floral decoration is permissible on all feast days when the frontal is white or red or green, and on such special occasions as baptism, confirmation, ordination, wedding (see Liturgical Calendar, Appendix VIII, page 203). Only long-keeping flowers should be used. They should be removed from the retable when they have begun to fade, and the empty vases should also be removed.

Design and Color

Good taste and consideration of the symbolic meaning of liturgical colors should lead an arranger to seek harmony in colors of flowers, and the Liturgical Calendar can be of great help in this respect.

The design of an altar arrangement should be in keeping with the architectural style of the church and convey the same general feeling. In placing plant material in a vase, try to lead attention toward the cross rather than carry the eye of the observer toward the outer ends of the altar. Keep the arrangement in proper scale with other appointments on the altar. No arrangement should appear bizarre, ostentatious, or in bad taste; that would be distracting to the congregation or the clergy.

In planning Christmas decoration for the church, if evergreen garlands or swags or loops are used, visualize their placement in such a way as to harmonize, not clash, with the church's main architectural lines and features.

In the second chapter of this book, reference is made to the ancient admonition of Pope Gregory (the Great) in his letter to St. Augustine, wherein the congregation is to be encouraged to enhance its place of worship with the beauty of flowers. Flowers and growing plants can lift our spirits in the way great music does, and the skillful, knowledgeable use of them in decorating a place of worship can, in a most subtle way, influence the spiritual nourishment of every worshiper. There can be no more devoted service to Deity, and it is counted an honor of high degree. The Reverend Dr. Nicholas Gihr, in his book *The Holy Sacrifice of the Mass*, has expressed this beautifully when he says:

"It should, then, be a loving occupation for us to adorn the church, to decorate the altar, and to enhance the beauty of divine worship with fresh and fragrant flowers. God is hereby honored, pious people are rejoiced and edified.

"The altar is here on earth the most holy and the most venerable of all places. To do honor to Him who here sacrifices Himself and who so graciously deigns to dwell among us, all the splendor and decoration of the temple lend their service. The altar, therefore, should be the most beautiful of all, and the pastor should have at heart, in a special manner, its adornment, so that he may in truth be able to say: 'I have loved, O Lord, the beauty of Thy house and the place where Thy glory dwelleth.' (Ps. 26:8)."

The Church Year

When planning unified decorations for the church, and to make them more meaningful, the arranger should be familiar with the church seasons and major feast days, and know why they are commemorated, how celebrated in the past, and something of the customs and legends that have grown up around them. A church calendar, with the liturgical colors blocked in and notation of the different feast days, is an invaluable reference aid.

Advent (four Sundays before December 25) marks the beginning of the church year. It is a time of preparation. Because Advent is a penitential season, the color for vestments and altar hangings is violet. In most churches, no flowers are used at this time, except on the third Sunday (Gaudete). The frontal for this day is rose. Roses and lilies are especially appropriate in floral arrangements. A shell symbolizes Advent and denotes baptism (*Matthew* 21).

An Advent wreath is a decoration used in many churches to depict the passing of time. The wreath is made of evergreens and around its rim, equidistant from each other, are placed four candles, one for each Sunday in Advent. One candle is lighted on each successive Sunday as Christmas draws near.

Christmastide (December 24 through Epiphany, January 6). This is a tender, loving, and holy season and is celebrated throughout the world as a joyous and happy one. As always, the altar is the most important center of interest in the church. Since Christmas is a major feast day, the frontal for it is white. Altar flowers may be white, red, pastel tints, silver, gold, with green of foliage. Garlands and wreaths should be planned to follow the architectural lines of the church. Candles may be used in the chancel and sanctuary. (See page 119 for instructions for making garlands, wreaths, swags.)

The poinsettia is called "the Christmas flower." Since it does not keep well in steam-heated buildings, when cut, it should be displayed in pots. These should be covered with dull green paper and banked with greens.

A Nativity scene may be placed in the church where children and adults can view it at close range. If boughs of evergreens are used with it, they should be in scale with the figures of the Holy Family and the animals. Such plant material as cryptomeria, arbor vitae, short-leaved fir, cedar, and others that may be used to simulate larger forms are suitable. Unadorned evergreen trees may be used in the chancel and about the sanctuary for decoration. A spotlight will show the trees to advantage. Sometimes a beautiful star placed at the uppermost tip of each tree can be very effective. The Christmas fir trees might be grown in tubs and later placed in the church garden.

Epiphany (January 6) commemorates the manifestation of Christ. The Magi brought the Child gifts of gold, frankincense, and myrrh. Frankincense (*Boswellia terifera*) is a woody shrub native to Palestine, from which an aromatic gum resin is produced. Myrrh (*Commiphora abyssinica*) also produces a resin and the plant is found in Africa, Asia, and the East Indies. These and other plants mentioned in the Bible might be cultivated in a church garden and used at Christmastide. Symbolically, the gold stood for kingly rights, the frankincense for priesthood; traditionally, the myrrh portended the death of Jesus.

The Christmas crèche is left in place in the church until after

Fig. 61. *Christmas Decorations for a Children's Party. Cookie Tree.* This triangular-shaped tree was made from a piece of plywood. Iced cookies of various shapes were attached to the plywood with boiled icing. The tree was then covered with cellophane. A bucket filled with cookies was placed to form the trunk of the tree.

Epiphany. The shepherds and sheep of the Nativity, however, are replaced by figures of the Wise Men.

To tie in with the royal gifts brought to the King of Kings, and with the deep feeling of the season, flowers used should be bright in color and rich in texture.

FIG. 62. *Christmas Decorations.* A soft, gold-colored metal was cut with scissors to form these six-pointed stars. Six red Christmas tree balls were grouped together to make the center of interest. These are effective as door or wall decorations.

The word Epiphany means manifestation or in modern interpretation, "enlightment." Since the star of Bethlehem brought light into men's lives, it is a symbol much loved and much used during Christmastide. It might be interesting to combine as many star-shaped flowers as possible in an arrangement for Epiphany. Since many gardens are dormant in January, bulbs such as paper-white narcissi, Star of Bethlehem, and the evergreen, vine-star jasmine could be started in pots for later cutting and arranging.

Eastertide or Paschal Time. The Easter cycle is movable, Easter Sunday occurring after the first full moon following the vernal equinox. Easter never occurs before March 22 nor later than April 25. It is the greatest of all Christian church festivals and is known in France as *Pasque*, in Spain as *Pascua*, in Italy as *Pasqua*. The season begins on

Photo Esther Wagner   *Fern Bowers Hunt*

FIG. 63. *Christmas Decorations.* A wreath made of evergreens and pine boughs is used to lead attention to the entrance of this building. The wreath follows the architectural lines of the semicircular door, while the pyramidal shrubs emphasize the long slender windows.

Ash Wednesday with Lent (40 days preceding Easter). This is a penitential season. The frontal is violet and no plant material is used in the church except on Palm Sunday, Maundy Thursday, and Laetare Sunday.

Palm Sunday is the Sunday preceding Easter. The frontal is again violet. Palms and olive branches may be used to decorate the church and are carried by the faithful in processions. In climates where palms and olives are not available, the willow may be substituted. The green of olive and palm connote a good Christian life. The palm symbolizes victory, grace, and mercy, while the olive denotes peace (*John* 12:13).

In Latin countries, tiny crosses are made by members of the altar guilds. These crosses are blessed and carried in procession. After the procession is over, the crosses should be returned to the church to be burned. The ashes are kept for the ensuing year, at which time they may be blessed. In many countries during a Palm Sunday procession, flowers are strewn on the streets before the oncoming clergy and laity. Palm and olive branches carried by the people are entwined with flowers. In France, roses are used with palm fronds.

Holy Thursday or Maundy Thursday is a day of both sadness and joy—sadness because of remembrance of Christ's Crucifixion and joy because He instituted the Blessed Sacrifice. The frontal is white, and flowers are used because they signify the Garden of Gethsemane. Lilies, dogwood, daffodils, roses, lilacs, peonies, narcissi, etc. are appropriate. A variety of colors in flowers may be used to decorate the High Altar and also a side altar.

Holy Saturday commemorates the burial of Jesus. At the vigil service in the evening, new fire is blessed and the solemn lighting of the Paschal Candle takes place. This lighted candle signifies the risen Christ and burns every Sunday until Ascension Day.

Easter Sunday celebrates Christ's Resurrection and is the true climax of joy and thanksgiving in the church year. The frontal is

Photo Russell Illig   *Fern Bowers Hunt*

Fig. 64. The symbolic meaning of this religious painting is emphasized by the placement of pine boughs and cones in various stages of development.

Photo Russell Illig   *Fern Bowers Hunt*

FIG. 65. Pleasing for any occasion is this contemporary type arrangement using the broad leaves of the hosta plant with the simple form of the dogwood blossoms. The lines in the leaves relate harmoniously to those of the dark green glass container. There is a perfect matching of colors here. A teakwood base is placed under the conical-shaped bowl to give a feeling of grace and balance.

white, and flowers are used in profusion. Lilies and roses are most often associated with Easter, but all flowers are welcome, provided they are in good condition and harmonious in color. Fragrant blooms are especially pleasing. If Easter lilies are used in pots, dull-finish paper concealing the pots is to be preferred to shiny metallic paper. If lilies are cut and combined with other flowers, the latter should conform in line, i.e., a pendulous rather than an upright one.

Pentecost or Whitsuntide occurs 50 days after Easter. It is a time of thanksgiving. Newly gathered fruits and grains of harmonious color are appropriate. On Pentecost Day, the baptismal font is blessed. Flowers may be banked at its base but are never placed in the font. A large candle, called the Illumination candle, may be lighted. On the Saturday after Pentecost, the Paschal season ends and Trinity Sunday follows.

Corpus Christi is celebrated on Thursday, 50 days after the Pentecost octave. It commemorates the institution of the Holy Eucharist on Maundy Thursday. It is celebrated at this later date because the faithful were still too sorrowful during Holy Week to give it the veneration fitting to it.

At Ginzano in Italy, a display of flowers, "Infiorata," is held this day on the steps of St. Mary's of the Summit. The procession passes over a mosaic carpet of flowers placed by children but designed by leading artists in the region. This sort of decoration is also found in other Latin countries. Often statues representing holy personages are carried in a procession over streets strewn with flowers.

The Assumption is the greatest feast honoring the Blessed Virgin Mary. In Europe at this time, plant material is brought to the church, and also to temporary altars set up in the fields, and is blessed. A statue of the Virgin is often taken to the fields, and there the farmers pray for good crops and good weather. Lilies and roses (the flowers of Mary) as well as the palm, are associated with the Virgin, but many other kinds may be used.

Photo William Arborgast

First Presbyterian Church, Palo Alto, Calif.

Fern Bowers Hunt

Appendix

I. The Workshop

It is said that a carpenter is as good as the tools he uses. This is likewise true for the arranger of plant materials. To save time and energy, the arranger must have good tools and a place to work that is comfortable and convenient. Perhaps you can improvise a workshop in the garage, utility room, or basement. Shelves may be added to give extra storage space and cupboards hung to hold equipment. Card tables may be set up when extra work space is required. If flower arrangement is to be one's hobby or avocation, as complete a workshop as possible is necessary. Ideally, the items listed should be included:

1. Cool, dark, dry room where freshly cut materials may be placed in deep cool water away from drafts. A place where lower parts of stems may be stripped of leaves. In this room, plant material may be treated with preservatives and plants hung for drying.

2. Shelf for preservatives:

Sugar	Tobacco
Salt	Gelatin
Alcohol	Alcohol lamp or candle
HCl	(for charring stems)
Vinegar	Floralife
Glycerin	Survival 77
Peppercorns	Aladdin Magic Flower Vitalizer

3. Open shelf for containers, big enough so they may be seen at a glance for selection as to color, contour, and line.

4. Cupboard for storing background materials:

Screens	Plaques	Niches
Mirrors	Trays	Hangings

5. Large worktable where arranger may be seated to compose arrangements.

6. Swivel chair.

7. Lazy Susan on which arrangements may be constructed and turned from side to side.

8. Drawer to hold flower frogs:

> Suction pin frog for wet container
> Variety of shapes and sizes in heavy frogs: daisy, pin, combination pin and daisy, other types
> Strips of lead
> Crumpled wire which may be impaled on heavy pin frog with piece of strong twig to take place of daisy holder

9. Shelf to hold decorative materials:

Gold paint	Adhesive tape
Silver paint	Adhesive bond
Bronze paint	Sequins
Christmas-tree balls, etc.	Ribbon
Lacquer (compressed air can)	Diamond dust
Magic snow (compressed air can)	

> Materials to cover pin frog: crushed rock and glass, marbles, shells, pebbles, moss

10. Shelf or table to hold cans of various sizes where flowers may be segregated as to size and color. This must be within reach of arranger.

11. Large shallow basket with handle to hold tools:

Sharp knife to cut stems at an angle	Razor blades to strip bark off lower stems
Clippers to cut heavy stems	Wire cutters
Scissors	Metal shears to cut metal

12. Another shallow, handled basket to hold:

> Florist's clay in various colors to anchor frog to dry container
> Materials for tying stems or for splicing and shaping stems:
>> Twistems (covered wire)
>> Fine wire, No. 28
>> Medium-size wire, No. 22, for inserting into hollow-stemmed plants for shaping
>> Pipe cleaners in variety of colors for tying
>> Small elastic bands for bunching slim stems
>> Cellophane tape

Items for impaling fruit, candy, seedpods, berries, Christmas-tree
balls, etc.
Toothpicks
Florist's pins
Sharp-pointed swabsticks (available at drugstores)
Stiff but pliable wire, No. 20

13. Square of plastic cloth, 56 x 56 inches, to use as floor cover.

II. Symbolism of Plant Materials

Plant	Significance
Acacia	Indestructible, deathless
Almond	Acceptable (*Numbers* 17:1–8)
Anemone	Trilobed leaves suggest the Trinity
	Red markings on petals, Christ's blood
	Thought to be the lilies of the field referred to in Christ's Sermon on the Mount
Apple (malum)	Original sin
	Apple in hand of Jesus denotes redemption
Arbutus	Hope
Aspen	Traditionally, the wood used for Christ's cross, therefore doomed to perpetual trembling
Azalea	Devotion
Bamboo	Friendship
Bedstraw	Manger bed of infant Jesus
Bleeding heart	Fidelity
Broom	Humility
Bulrush	Living waters, constancy (*Job* 8:11)
Camellia	Purity, contentment
Camomile	Courage
Carnation	Love, if red; nuptials, if pink
Cedar	Constancy (*Song of Solomon* 5:15). Because of its height, longevity, healing qualities, fragrance, it was related to the greatness and goodness of Mary
Cherry	Chivalry (fruit of Paradise)
Chestnut	Burrs suggest the crown of thorns
Christmas Rose (Hellebore)	Abnegation, selflessness
Chrysanthemum	Modesty
Clematis	Hardihood, ruggedness

Plant	*Significance*
Clover	Trilobed leaves suggest the Trinity
	In Ireland called the shamrock, symbolizing good luck
Cockleburrs	Weakness (*Job* 31:40)
Columbine	Seven spurs resemble doves
	Attributes of human heart: wisdom, counsel, understanding, knowledge, piety, fear of the Lord (*Isaiah* 11:2)
Corn ears	Eucharist
Cornflower	Love
Cyclamen	Bleeding nun
	Mary's sorrows
Cypress	Death, because it does not grow again from roots when cut
	Shape points heavenward, emblem of Virgin Mary
Daffodil	Joy, devotion
Daisy	Innocence, youth, simplicity
Dandelion	Wisdom
Dogwood	Penitence
	Also said to be wood of Christ's cross
Elm	Strength, protectiveness
Ferns	Humility, grace, and beauty
Fig	Lust, fertility (*Genesis* 3:7), life
Fir	Prosperity (because it is evergreen)
Fleur-de-lis or Fleur de lys	Purity, associated with Virgin Mary
(flower of the lily)	Three were fixed on medieval French battle arms in honor of the Trinity
	(See also Lily, Lily of the valley)
Forget-me-not	Love, faith and hope
Fruit	Fruits of Spirit: love, joy, longsuffering, peace, goodness, gentleness, faithfulness, meekness, patience, temperance, modesty, chastity
	Any fruit depicted in the hands of St. Catherine denoted fruits of the Spirit: joy, peace, love
Gardenia	Purity
Gentian	Hope
Gourd	Resurrection (*Jonah* 4)
Grain	Eucharist body of Christ (*John* 12:24)

Plant	*Significance*
Grape	Holy Sacrament, blood of Christ
Hawthorn	Devotion, when carried in wedding ceremony
Holly	Crown of thorns, protection
Hyacinth	Constancy
Hyssop	Purity (*Psalm 51:7*)
Iris (sword lily)	Sorrow of Mary (see also Fleur-de-lis)
Ivy	Immortality (evergreen)
Jasmine	Flower of Mary, because of fragrance
Laurel	Victory, eternity (*I Corinthians 9:24–27*)
Lemon	Love and fidelity
Lily	Innocence, purity, virginity, Immaculate Conception, the sun, redemption
	Attribute of Archangel Gabriel
Lotus	Truth, purity
Magnolia	Virtue
Myrtle	Love, peace, long life (*Isaiah 55:12–13*)
Narcissus	Self-love, also triumph of divine love over selfishness
Oak	Strength, endurance
Olive	God's goodness (*Judges 9:8–9*)
Olive branch	Peace, hope, abundance
Orange blossom	Purity
Orange tree	Generosity
Palm	Victory over death (*John 12:12–13*)
	Sign of martyr's grave
	Emblem of Virgin Mary
Pansy	Remembrance
Peach	Wisdom, silence
Pear	Christ's love
Pine	Strength, loyalty, endurance, longevity, prosperity
Plane tree	Charity
Plantain	Waybread
Plum	Fidelity
Plum tree	Vitality, because it blooms before leafing out
Pomegranate	Many seeds, unity of Church, also hope and resurrection
	Bud end resembles crown, denotes royalty
Poppy	Forgetfulness
Reed	Greatness

Plant	*Significance*
Rose	Queen of flowers, flower of Virgin Mary
	Victory, triumph, love, pride, martyrdom, beauty
	During Middle Ages, when suspended over conference table, signified all that was said must be kept secret (*sub rosa*)
	In early Christian times, roses were given as gifts on Laetare Day (fourth Sunday in Lent) because they denote both rejoicing and suffering, having beauty and fragrance, but also thorns. The Golden Rose was blessed by the Pope on this day, at which time he gave a discourse on its symbolism
Strawberry	Trilobed leaves signify the Trinity; red fruit, the martyrs
Syringa	Fidelity
Thistle	Sorrow (*Genesis* 3:17–18)
Thorn	Grief
Tree	Denotes life, if it is strong (*Genesis* 2:9), death, if it is a weakling
Tree, stem, rod of Jesse	Genealogy of family (*Isaiah* 11:1–2), progeny
	Stem of Jesse symbolized by branch entwined with flowers
Vine	God's love for His children (*Isaiah* 5:7; *John* 15:1, 5, 8)
Violet	Humility, penitence, modesty
Wheat	Bread of Life (Christ's body), Eucharist
Willow	Unyielding, because it is flexible but strong
Yew	Immortality

III. Symbolism of Objects and Other Attributes in Church Decoration

Object	Significance
Altar	Represents Christ's sacrifice (*Ephesians* 2:20)
Anchor	Used by early Christians to signify cross
	Steadfastness, undying hope
Anvil	Death
Arrow	Ardent love when piercing object
Ashes	Abasement
Aureole	Bright light surrounding only members of Godhead
Axe	Martyrdom
	Object used by St. Boniface to fell the German sacred oak, thereby presenting his faith in things Christian to the irate pagans who worshiped the god Thor
Banner	Victory
Basin and ewer	Condoning crime (*Matthew* 27:24)
Beehive	Fluency, thrift
Blood	Eucharist, sacrifice
Book	Knowledge
Candelabrum	Seven-branched: Christ, the light of the world
	Seven gifts of the Holy Spirit (*Revelation* 1:20)
Carbuncle	Red blood, the five wounds of Christ
Chalice and Host	Eucharist, Holy
Church edifice	Love and protection
Circles (three joined)	Eternity, wholeness, Trinity
Clouds	God's omnipresence

Object	Significance
Cross	Symbol of Christianity; replaced fish symbol after Emperor Constantine gave Christians right to public worship
Crown	Honor
Crown of thorns	Christ's Passion
Crucifix	Hope, fidelity, penance, symbol of Christ's suffering
Darkness	The devil
Dawn	Blood of Christ
Ear	Word of God
Earth	Shelter, protectiveness
East	Christ
Eye	Enlightenment, God all-seeing
Fire	Ardor
Fisherman's net	The Church
Font	Humility (*John* 13:5), regeneration
Fountain	Life eternal
Garden	Gethsemane
Gold	Idolatry, riches
Hand	Denotes God, when depicted issuing through clouds
Hands (pair)	God, fidelity
Harbor	Eternal life
Heart	Guides the mind for good
Honey	Goodness
Keys	Spiritual power
Ladder	Descent from the cross
Lamp	Enlightenment (*Psalm* 119:105; *John* 8:12)
Lantern	Betrayal, Judas
Letters	IHS, Greek symbols for Jesus Christ, King of Kings (not *Iesus Hominus Salvator*, as previously thought)
	I.N.R.I., Latin, signifying *Iesus Nazarenus, Rex Iudacorum* (Jesus of Nazareth, King of the Jews)
Lyre	Harmony
Mirror	Image of goodness and justice, truth
Moon	Symbol of Virgin Mary (*Song of Solomon* 6:10)
	("A woman [meaning the Virgin Mary] clothed with the sun, and the moon under her feet, and upon her head a crown of twelve stars.")

Object	*Significance*
Nails	Passion
North	Darkness, forboding
Oil (chrism)	Anointing. The name Christ comes from Latin *chrisma*
Pillar and cord	Scourging of Jesus
Pearl	Word of God (*Matthew* 13:45)
Pitch	Sin, death
Rainbow	Last Judgment (*Revelation* 4:2–5), promise
Ring	Fidelity, eternity
River	Four Gospels, refreshment
Robe	Passion
Rock	St. Peter ("Thou art Peter, and upon this rock I will build my church." (*Matthew* 16:18), firmness
Salt	Superiority (*Matthew* 5:13)
Scales	Justice
Seven	A sacred number
	Seven doves, gifts of the Holy Spirit: wisdom, counsel, strength, knowledge, understanding, piety, holy fear
	Seven sacraments
	Seven planets
	Seven days of week
	Seven liberal arts
	Seven-branch candelabra
	Seven churches of Asia
	Seven joys of the Virgin: annunciation; visitation; adoration of Magi; presentation in the Temple; Christ found by Mary talking to the doctors; the Assumption; coronation
	Seven sorrows of the Virgin: the prophecy of Simeon; flight into Egypt; Christ lost; betrayal of Christ; the Crucifixion; descent from the cross; Ascension
	Seven canonical hours
	Seven chants and amens (sevenfold amen)
	Seven chapels, as in Amiens and Chartres cathedrals
Shell	Baptism, pilgrimage
Ship (navis)	Church
Silver	Pure as silver (*Psalm* 12:6)

Object	Significance
Skull	Penance
Smoke	(*Psalm 74:1*)
Square	The earth
Star	Guided the Magi, symbol of promise, merit
Stones	Firmness
Sun	Christ
Sword	Weapon for good, valor
Triangle	Trinity
Water	Purifier (*Matthew 27:24*)
Well	Eternal life
Wings	Angels

BIRDS, BEASTS, AND FISH

Object	Significance
Ass	Nativity, flight into Egypt, triumphal journey of Christ into Jerusalem on first Palm Sunday, patience
Dog	Good and evil, faithful and contemptible (*Isaiah 56:10*)
Dolphin	Resurrection, bearer of souls to isle of the dead, pleasure
Dove	Holy Spirit, purity, innocence, chastity, inspiration
	Dove emitting bright rays denotes the Trinity, peace
	Seven doves, gifts of the Holy Spirit
	Twelve doves, symbolic of the twelve apostles
	Twelve days of Christmas
Dragon	Satan, heresy defeated, sin
Eagle	Lofty flight refers to the apostles, more especially to John the Baptist because of his keen vision to see spiritually
	Ascension, Last Judgment, liberty
Elephant	Sin
Fish	ICHTHYS, Greek abbreviation for *Iesous Christos Theou Hyios Soter* (Jesus Christ, Son of God, Saviour). Therefore a fish first symbolized Christ during the period of Christian persecution
	Also symbolic of baptism, one standing for Christ, more than one Christian, St. Peter

Object	*Significance*
Fox	Satan's treachery (*Luke* 13:32)
Hen	Loving care (*Matthew* 23:37)
Lamb	Christ, St. Agnes, meekness, innocence (*Isaiah* 53:7; *Revelation* 6:16, 17; *John* 1:29)
Lion	Assigned to Christ because of royal dignity (*Psalms* 121:4)
	Winged lion emblem of St. Mark (*Ezekiel* 1:10–14; *Mark* 1:3; *I Peter* 5:8)
Ox	Nativity, nobility, strength (*Luke* 2:14)
	Winged ox symbolizes St. Luke, also atonement made by Christ's Passion, priesthood of Christ
Peacock	Immortality, earthly pride (*I Corinthians* 2:9)
Pelican	Christ on the cross (*Psalm* 102:6)
Phoenix	Resurrection of Jesus
Rabbit	Christians, fertility
Rooster	Light and faith
Serpent	Evil (*Genesis* 3:1, 14)
Sheep	Twelve apostles of Christ (Christ the Shepherd) (*John* 10:11)
Stag	Baptism (*Psalm* 41), solitude
Swallows	Loving care
Unicorn	Christ, also female chastity

SYMBOLS OF THE EVANGELISTS

Object	*Significance*
Cherub	St. Matthew
Heavenly flight	St. John
Lion	St. Mark
Ox	St. Luke

SYMBOLS OF THE APOSTLES

Object	*Significance*
Carpenter's ruler	St. Thomas
Chalice with serpent	St. John
Club	St. James (minor)
Cross	St. Philip
Cross that bears his name	St. Andrew
Halberd	St. Simon or Thaddeus
Keys or fish	St. Peter
Knife	St. Bartholomew
Lance	St. Matthias
Purse	St. Matthew
Staff	St. James (major)

IV. Color Connotation for Christian Churches

Black: Mourning, death, Satan, temptation, wickedness
Blue: Truth, fidelity, constancy, humility, heaven, divine love, association with Virgin Mary. Blue forbidden for vestments (Catholic)
Gold: Goodness, fruitfulness, preciousness, rarity, divinity
Gray: Penance, mourning, humility
Green: Longevity, hope, prosperity, new growth, eternity, immortality
Orange: Energy, warmth, well-being; never used in altar floral arrangement but appropriate in informal church rooms
Purple: Penance; secular connotation is royalty, nobility, pomp and circumstance
Red: Martyrdom, royalty, fire, loyalty, love, wisdom; also connotes war, hatred, purgatory, Satan
Violet: Penance, sorrow, passion, suffering
White: Purity, chastity, innocence, faith, felicity, joy; principal color for great festivals of church year (however, in some Oriental religions, white is the color of mourning)
Yellow: Jealousy, hypocrisy, inconstancy, deceit (Judas); less appropriate for altar arrangements but is lively and gay in less formal compositions. Forbidden for vestments (Catholic)
(See liturgical colors for decorating High Altar in church calendar, Appendix VII, page 203.)

V. Christmas Customs

Australia

Australians use peacocks in their Christmas decorations. They place the stuffed birds, with tails spread and beaks gilded, on their dinner tables. The ugly feet are concealed with greens.

Austria

St. Nicholas' Day is celebrated in Austria on December 5 to commemorate this saint's generosity and kindness to the poor. Instead of a Santa Claus bearing gifts, a young man is chosen by the people to represent the Bishop of Myra, who preaches a short sermon and distributes gifts to the children.

Brittany (France)

On the evening of Christmas Day the people of small villages build campfires and set candles in the windows to lead the Holy Family to their homes. The table is spread in readiness for them, with coarse bread and milk. Should the wind be blowing during this time, it portends wind for every day of the year.

Czechoslovakia

In this country, a fine symmetrical tree is set up in the house, and cookies made in the shapes of Christmas symbols hung on it. The symbols are fish, crowns, bells, flowers, fruit, and animals.

Denmark

Two large candles are set in the window of each home to guide the Christ Child to it. One candle represents the master, the other the mistress of the house. Each is lighted by the oldest member of the family living in the house. The candles burn from Christmas morning until New Year's Day.

England

Kissing boughs (or kissing balls) are made of greens, mistletoe, and apples; gifts are placed in them and they are hung in doorways. Whoever stands under one may be kissed. Evergreen garlands decorate the yule log, which is lighted from last year's log. This is kept burning during the entire Christmas season up to Twelfth Night, January 6. Pieces of the yule log are kept as charms against lightning, and one to light next year's log.

France

On Christmas Eve the children put their shoes *(sabots)* on the hearth, hoping Father Christmas will fill them during the night. In the morning, the children are given cookies decorated thickly with icing depicting crowns, stars, dragons, and the Three Kings.

In Alsace-Lorraine, a legend is told to the children about a little girl called *Christ Kind* who went from door to door distributing gifts to the needy. She wore a crown on her head, carried a bell in her hand and a basket on her arm which contained gifts. She was said to be the Christ Child masquerading as the little girl.

Another legend is related about the shepherds who brought gifts to the baby Jesus at Bethlehem. One brought a rattle made from a dead weed which, when shaken, made the seeds rattle. Another brought a lambkin skin for warmth; a third brought a field daisy. The daisy was held for the baby to see, and the story goes that He touched it with His lips and the petals turned red at the edges, thereby portending His death on Calvary.

The children write letters at Christmas time to *Cher Papa Noel* and ask for presents.

In the city of Rouen, The Crib *(Officium Pastorum)* meaning Office of the Shepherd is celebrated in drama form. The most moving of all the Christmas the Missa in Nocte (during the night, corresponding to our Christmas Eve midnight services), which symbolizes the eternal birth of the Word of God in the Father; the Missa in Aurora (dawn) celebrating the birth of God in the flesh, and the Missa in Die (during the day), the birth of Jesus in the hearts of His followers.

Germany

It is said that St. Boniface went to Germany to convert the heathen to Christianity. He cut down their sacred oak, the pagans were enraged, and therefore he offered to replace the oak with a fir tree as a symbol of his faith. In the night, it was said, a spider spun a shining web in and out and over the tree. Icicles formed on it and when the sun came out the next morning the tree glittered and sparkled, causing the people to rejoice and to embrace Christianity. The icicle tree continues to be their symbol of Christmas. A different version of the legend tells about the stars that shone through the tree and brought about conversions from paganism to Christianity.

In southern Germany, the people hang cookies and candies of various shapes on little trees. They also put corn and other grain on the roof tops for the birds. They fill mangers with an extra supply of hay for the cattle and sheep, in gratefulness to these animals for sharing their mangers with the Holy Family at Bethlehem.

In northern Germany, the people wrap little figures for gifts, called *julklapp*, in many pieces of paper. One figure is of an old woman, the other of an old man. They are believed to bring good luck to the recipient.

In the village of Berchtesgaden (Bavaria), the bishop visits the homes of his parishioners. He is accompanied by a boy dressed as a girl and twelve masked boys dressed in straw suits. They carry cowbells which they shake, presumably to drive out evil spirits. The masquerading boy (*Nikolo-Weibl*) distributes gifts to the children while the twelve young men (*Buttenmandln*) drive the people from their homes, a practice which is supposed to bring good luck to everyone.

In the regions where there are herds, Tyrol milk is left on the doorstep for the Christ Child, who may need refreshment as He passes by.

Holland

The children stuff their wooden shoes with straw and red apples, and place them outside for the horses at Christmas.

India

Nativity scenes are set up in Christian churches. Red brick is used for the crib, and it is decorated with garlands of greens, flowers, and colored paper streamers.

In Bengal, ferns, flowers, and silk ribbons are used to decorate the churches.

Ireland

Large candles are placed in windows during the Christmas season, to guide the Christ Child. In ancient times, a death at Christmas time was considered a blessing, as the people presumed that the pearly gates stood wide open then to Christian and sinner alike.

Italy

Presents are distributed by a *Befana* (female Santa Claus) on Epiphany Eve. In ancient days, the children were warned that if they misbehaved the *Befana* would carry them away. Today the children write letters to their patron saint.

In Florence, a festival is held on January 6. It is celebrated with bonfires, the blowing of trumpets, and singing of sacred songs while the people march in procession.

St. Francis of Assisi instigated tableau scenes, with live people and animals depicting the Nativity. He did this to impress more deeply on the people the true significance of Christmas, for, as he said, "seeing is worth a thousand words." As interest grew in these Nativity tableaus, wood carvers made little scenes of them and are still making and selling them today.

In some churches in Italy, the crib (*presepio*) is lavishly decorated with jewels, greens, flowers, and gay-colored ribbons. The *Bambino* is kissed to show the world that Christianity has triumphed over paganism, and customs that were once pagan are turned to Christian use. In pre-Christian times, the people celebrated the winter solstice (*Saturnalia*) by decorating their homes, statues, and temples with greens and flowers made into garlands and wreaths. It is said they lashed one another with green whips to bring good luck. Today the people merely exchange green boughs as tokens of good luck.

Ad Proesepe (To the Crib) is celebrated in pageantry at Christmas at St. Mary Major called the Station. In ancient days, all the dignitaries assisted in it. Candles were lighted around the church by the Pope, and flax placed high on columns was also ignited, to signify the coming of Christ.

Every household in Italy celebrates Christmas by having a crèche or crib in its midst. Around the tiny manger are placed finely carved figures of the Holy Family and domestic animals. These are set in a simulated pastoral background. The father of the family makes the *presepio*.

The Italians light a great log (*ceppo*) on Christmas night, and while they sit together as families, they tell the children all the interesting things that have happened to the family.

Mexico

A drama called *Las Posadas* is held in certain homes on Christmas Eve (*Noche Buena*). Statues of Joseph and Mary are carried through the streets and to various homes by two people chosen to represent these Holy People. Children trail the procession. The adults carry lighted candles, presumably searching for the *Nacimiento* (manger bed). At last a door is opened and it is found. An image of the Christ Child is placed in the crib and the people sing carols and offer up prayers. To conclude the celebration, a *piñata*, which is an earthen vessel or papier-mâché container sometimes in the shape of an animal, is filled with sweets, fruits, and small presents and hung from the ceiling. The children strike at the vessel with a bat or a stick until it is broken and the presents spill out. There are gifts for everyone, and each child must wait patiently until they are all distributed.

Poinsettias and Madonna lilies are used to decorate churches and homes and also the processional vehicles that transport the statues from one place to another.

Norway

A candle is lighted on Christmas Eve in each home and is extinguished in the morning. This is continued during the season, to Epiphany. Only the heads of families are allowed to touch the candle, as it is considered bad luck for others to do so.

Julotte is a custom that takes place in the church parish house on Christmas Eve. People wait during the night, singing carols and praying in the candlelit room. As day dawns, each person lights a candle to hold, and all stand in a circle and wish one another a happy Christmas.

The Philippines

Here the people hold a celebration called *Las Misas de Aguinaldo* (Preparation) at which band music is played very early in the morning.

Poland

Young people dressed in native costume go from house to house singing carols. At each stopping-place they are invited in and given sweets and hot cider. Extra portions of food are put out to feed the animals. The houses and parish houses are decorated with sheaves of wheat and cornstalks as protection against evil spirits. Tables are spread with white cloths and on each is placed a decoration made of straw, representing the Christ Child's bed. The food served has a Christian symbolic connotation. Little wafers are served before the supper as a memorial of love to the Christ Child.

Scotland

The people usher in the New Year by swinging tallow-coated ropes called fireballs. In the country, farmers fire off guns to bring good luck in crops and weather.

The people also celebrate Epiphany (January 6), which they call Hoagmany, meaning season. They sing and dance to the music of bagpipes.

Shetland Islands

Lerwick Day is celebrated on January 13. It is called the Festival of Fire, or Helly-on. A Norse galley is dragged through the streets on wheels, accompanied by young men in Norseman costumes, carrying lighted torches. They invite the spectators to join in the singing of Norse songs. Lighted torches are thrown from the galley and whoever catches the burning fag-

FIG. 66. *Golden Wedding Decoration.* Golden Emblem roses repeat the spherical form of the gold-incrusted glass container. An amber glass fan, in a traditional pattern, completes and unifies the composition.

gots tosses them back. This is to insure good luck for the coming year. If the bunch of faggots falls to the ground, one's luck is supposed to fail for that year.

Silesia (former Prussian provinces)

Peasants carry grain to church on Christmas Day to have it blessed. Afterward, it is fed to the poultry to ward off sickness among the fowls.

Spain

Gifts are distributed on Epiphany. According to Spanish tradition, it is the Wise Men or Magi who bring them, rather than Santa Claus. Men go out from the churches to seek the Wise Men, who come riding in on camels. Bells are rung and torches lighted to show them the way. Children stand at candlelit windows to welcome the Magi when they come. The children fill their shoes with straw and place them on the doorstep for the camels. A little straw is also lighted as the Wise Men pass. Presents are

Photo Esther Wagner   *Members of the Altar Guild*

FIG. 67. *St. Thomas Aquinas Catholic Church, Palo Alto, Calif.* The green branches of the huckleberry shrub are effective against the beautiful white marble of this traditional style altar. The dark color of the leaves also ties to the beautiful circular window and the woodwork of the church.

distributed by the Three Kings to those children who have not misbehaved
badly during the year.

Sweden

On December 13, Little Yule, a feast of lights, is celebrated. Every
parish in the villages selects a young girl, a Lucia Bride, as a queen to rule
during the Christmas season. She is dressed in white and wears a crown
of greens in which lighted candles are placed. She has many young girls
as attendants who are called "star boys."

Before people are awake, she and her helpers prepare food and take it
to the various homes in their vicinity, singing as they go. They also visit
cow byres and stables and offer straw to the animals. This insures an
abundance of food to both people and animals during the coming year.

Presents are distributed on St. Lucia's day. The *julkapp*, wrapped in
many layers of paper, is presented unexpectedly. The person who brings
it opens the door unannounced, throws the gift inside, and departs quickly.
For the gift to be appreciated and effective, the donor must remain un-
known.

The Swedish people, like those in many other countries, also leave corn
and other grain on stable and house roofs for wild birds.

Switzerland

On December 5 a young man, dressed as a bishop to represent St. Nicholas, preaches a sermon on how children should behave. Then he hears the
children recite their catechism. If they fail, no presents. Sometimes children are told that they may be put in a servant's sack and taken away to
Spain. Despite these admonitions, the children love St. Nicholas and are
eager to see him.

Syria

On the evening before Christmas, a family may lock its gates and form
a procession outside, each carrying a lighted candle. They then go to a
place where an unlit bonfire has been prepared. The youngest son reads
from the Bible and the father lights the bonfire. Each member of the family watches the flames to see if they will show the way to good luck during
the coming year. When the fire burns low each person, one by one, jumps
over the dying embers and makes a wish. All then sing hymns around
the dying fire.

Early the next morning, another bonfire is lighted and the family follow a chosen member as he carries a figure of the Christ Child around
the blaze. Then he touches each member in the circle with the image (the
touch of peace) which symbolizes that they will live together in peace.

Wales

The Welsh people are known throughout the world for their fine singing, particularly at Christmas time. *Plygain,* or Crowing of the Cock, is observed during the Christmas season. The church is decorated with colored candles for a four o'clock service. The young men of the church, carrying lighted torches, accompany the minister to the church for a service of prayer and music.

VI. Selected Lists of Plant Materials

(A) Spike Forms, (B) Rounded Forms, (C) Drooping Habit of Growth, (D) Cup or Funnel-Shaped Forms, (E) Filler Material, (F) Dominant Material for Formal and Informal Weddings, (G) Subordinate Material for Formal and Informal Weddings, (H) Fragrant Flowers, (I) Star-Shaped Flowers (5 or 6 Petals), (J) Suitable for Drying, (K) Suitable for Corsages.

A. SPIKE FORMS

Acanthus
Aconitum (monkshood)
Aloe
Alstroemeria
Astilbe
Bellflower
Bridal wreath
Broom
Buddleia
Campanula pyramidalis
Carpathian harebell
Delphinium
Flax
Flowering fruit trees
Flowering quince
Forsythia
Foxglove
Francoa ramosa
Fremontia
Gladiolus
Goldenrod
Heather
Hollyhock
Kniphofia

Larkspur
Lavender
Leptospermum
Liatris
Lilac
Lupine
Montbretia
Mullein
Penstemon
Philadelphus
Phlox
Physostegia
Salvia
Snapdragon
Stock
Sweet rocket
Tamarix
Thernopsis
Tritoma
Wallflower
Weigela
Willow
Yucca

B. ROUNDED FORMS

Abutilon (flowering maple)
African daisy
Agapanthus
Anemone
Aster
Azalea
Bachelor button
Balloon flower
Begonia (tuberous)
Bush poppy
Calendula
California poppy
Calochortus
Camellia
Candytuft
Canna
Carnation
Christmas rose (hellebore)
Cineraria
Clarkia
Clematis
Clivia
Cockscomb
Cosmos
Crape myrtle
Dahlia
Daisy
Dianthus
Dogwood
Gaillardia
Gardenia
Godetia
Hibiscus
Hydrangea
Iceland poppy
Marguerite
Marigold
Ornithogalum
Pansy
Pasque flower
Passion flower
Pelargonium
Peony
Poinsettia
Poppy
Primrose
Ranunculus
Rose
Salpiglossis
Scabiosa
Shirley poppy
Sweet William
Transvaal daisy
Trollius
Tuberose
Tulip
Tulip tree
Zinnia

C. DROOPING HABIT OF GROWTH

Acacia
Ailanthus
Alyssum saxatile
Bergenia
Billbergia
Bittersweet
Bleeding-heart
Bougainvillea
Bouvardia
Chinese lantern
Columbine
Cup-and-saucer vine
Cup of gold vine
Currant
Cyclamen
Daffodil
Fuchsia
Golden chain tree
Grapes
Honeysuckle
Jasmine
Lantana

Mattress vine
Mountain laurel
Nasturtium
Orchid
Pepper berries
Periwinkle
Philadelphus
Ribes
Rosemary
Sand verbena
Silk-tassel tree

Smilax
Snowball bush
Snowberry
Star jasmine
Stephanotis
Strawberry tree
Trumpet vine (bignonia)
Verbena
Virginia creeper
Wandering jew
Wisteria

D. CUP OR FUNNEL-SHAPED FORMS

Abutilon
Agapanthus
Amaryllis
Anthurium
Balloon flower
Bell flower
Bergenia
Bouvardia
Calla
Calochortus
Canna
Christmas rose
Clarkia
Clivia
Columbine
Convolvulus (morning glory)
Coral-bells
Coral vine
Cup-and-saucer vine
Cup of gold vine

Daffodil
Day lily
Erythronium lily
Fuchsia
Globe tulip
Godetia
Hibiscus
Hollyhock
Hosta
Iris
Lilies (all)
Magnolia grandiflora
Narcissus
Nasturtium
Nicotiana
Petunia
Salpiglossis
Sweet pea
Tigridia
Trumpet vine (bignonia)

E. FILLER MATERIAL

Abelia
Acacia
Ageratum
Ailanthus
Alyssum saxatile
Beauty bush
Bleeding-heart
Bougainvillea

Bouvardia
Canary bush
Candytuft
Cape forget-me-not
Choisya
Chrysanthemum (button)
Cineraria
Cornflower (bachelor button)

Correa
Cotoneaster
Currant
Cynoglossum
Dahlia (button)
Daisy (Swan River)
Daphne
Deutzia
Diosma
Dogwood
Elderberry
Eryngium
Escallonia
Eucalyptus (flowering)
Fairy primrose
Floribunda rose
Forget-me-not
Freesia
Fringe tree
Fritillaria
Fuchsia (small)
Geranium
Glory-of-the-snow
Grape hyacinth
Gypsophila
Hawthorn
Heather
Hellebore
Heuchera (coral-bells)
Jasmine (star)
Kolwitzia
Lantana
Lavender
Leucojum

Lily of the valley
Lobelia
Love-in-a-mist
Matricaria
Meadow rue
Mimulus
Montbretia
Oleander
Osmanthus
Philadelphus
Photinia
Plumbago
Polianthes tuberosa
Primula
Redbud
Schizanthus
Scilla
Scotch broom
Sea lavender
Service berry
Snowdrop
Sweet alyssum (saxatile)
Sweet pea
Sweet violet
Syringa
Tamarix
Thalictrum
Verbena
Viburnum
Viola
Witch hazel
Yarrow
Zauschneria

F. DOMINANT MATERIAL FOR WEDDINGS

(These are merely guideline lists, not intended for strict adherence.)

Formal	*Informal*
Amaryllis	African daisy
Amazon lily	Aster
Anthurium	Calendula
Begonia, tuberous	Chrysanthemum
Calla lily	Cosmos

Formal	Informal
Camellia	Dahlia
Carnation	Daisy
Cattleya orchid	Day lily
Clematis	Dogwood
Clivia	Gaillardia
Cymbidium	Geranium
Epiphyllum	Hibiscus
Gardenia	Hollyhock
Gladiolus florets	Hydrangea
Gloriosa lily	Marigold
Hemerocallis (day lily)	Petunia, ruffled
Hibiscus	Poinsettia
Lily	Poppy
Peony	Ranunculus
Rhododendron florets	Sweet William
Spathyphyllum	Tigridia
Tulip	Tulip
Water lily	Tulip tree (flower)
	Yucca
	Zinnia

G. SUBORDINATE MATERIAL FOR WEDDINGS

(These are merely guideline lists, not intended for strict adherence.)

Formal	Informal
Agapanthus	Acacia
Andromeda	Agapanthus florets
Anemone	Ageratum
Azalea	Alstroemeria
Bougainvillea	Alyssum saxatile
Bouvardia	Andromeda
Cyclamen	Anemone
Cymbidium (orchid)	Astilbe
Daffodil (white)	Babys-breath (gypsophila)
Dendrobium	Bridal wreath
Dianthus	Coral-bells
Freesia	Cornflower
Fuchsia	Cosmos
Galanthus (snowdrop)	Dahlia (button)
Gladiolus (miniature)	Daisy (small)
Hyacinth	Daphne
Iris	Delphinium
Lilac	Dogwood

Formal	*Informal*
Lily of the valley	Euphorbia
Narcissus	Feverfew
Orange blossom	Forget-me-not
Ornithogalum	Freesia
Primrose (fairy)	Fuchsia
Rose (floribunda or	Gerbera
polianthus roses)	Geum
Scilla	Goldenrod
Snowdrop	Grape hyacinth
Stephanotis	Hellebore
Tuberose	Hyacinth
Watsonia	Iris
Wisteria	Jasmine
	Larkspur
	Lilac
	Marguerite
	Meadow rue
	Mock orange
	Mountain laurel
	Nicotiana
	Pinks
	Primrose
	Pyrethrum
	Queen Anne's lace
	Scabiosa
	Shasta daisy
	Snapdragon
	Spiraea
	Stock
	Thalictrum (meadow rue)
	Verbena
	Viburnum
	Violet
	Wallflower
	Wisteria
	Zinnia (small)

H. FRAGRANT FLOWERS

Azalea	Azara (microphylla)
American natives:	Balloon flower (plicata)
mucronatum	Banana shrub
roseum	Bouvardia (humboldii albatross)
vacasum	Broom (*see* Cytisus)

Buckthorn
Buddleja (davidi)
Camellia
  fragrans
  Sasanqua
    apple blossom
    Rosea
Carnation
Choisya (ternata)
Clematis (Armandii)
Columbine, long spur
Crab apple
Currant, flowering
Cytisus
  canariensis
  fragrans
Daffodil
  odorus
  poetaz
Daphne
  gnidium
  odora
Dianthus
  caressus
  Caryophyllus
  plumarius
Erysimum
Forsythia
Freesia (refracta alba)
Gardenia (jasmodii)
Genista (*see* Cytisus)
Geranium
Gladiolus
Honeysuckle
Hyacinth
Iris
  graminea
Jasmine
  grandiflorum
  magnificum
  officinale
Jonquilla odorus
Laurel (English)

Lavendula
Lilac
Lily
  auratum
  regale
  Washington
Lily of the valley
Locust
Loquat
Magnolia
  grandiflora
  Wilsonii
Mahonia bealeii
Mimosa
Nicotiana (alata)
Onosma (stellulatum)
Ornithogalum (star of Bethlehem)
  arabicum
Osmanthus
  Fortunei
  fragrans
  ilicifolius
Paeonia
Pelargonium
Petunia
Philadelphus
  cordifolius
  virginales
Poinciana
Primrose
  Barrowby Gem
  florida
  sikkincensis
Rhododendron
Ribes (currant)
Rose
Scotch broom
Skimmia (japonica)
Star jasmine
Stephanotis (floribunda)
Stock (winter)
Sweet pea
Sweet rocket

Syringa (lilac)   Burkwoodii
Tulip   carcephalum
 syvestris   Wormwood
Viburnum   Yucca

I. STAR-SHAPED FLOWERS (5 OR 6 PETALS)

Agapanthus   Lilies
Azalea (schlippenbachi)   Lithospermum (prostratium)
Azara   Mentzelia
Campanula   Narcissi (paper white)
 latifolia   Potentilla (gold drop)
 persifolia   Star jasmine
 rotundifolia   Star of Bethlehem
Columbine   Stephanotis
Deutzia (elegantisima)   Viburnum
Hypericum   carcephalum
 Hidcote   fragrans
 Sungold   Weigela

J. SUITABLE FOR DRYING

Symbols for treating materials:

UPS · Upside-down method: hang in cool dark place to dry. Good air circulation necessary for success with these materials.

UP   Arrange in dry container. Let dry away from light.

PM   Peatmoss or vermiculite method. (See page 115.)

GLYC Glycerin method: let stand in solution of 1 part glycerin, 2 parts water for from 2 to 6 weeks.

Acacia UP   Astilbe UPS
Acanthus UP   Babys-breath (Gypsophila) UP
Agave UP   Bamboo UP
Aloe UP   Banksia UP
Alyssum Saxatile UP   Barberry UP
Anemone PM   Barley (bearded) UP
Anise UP   Bayberry UP
Anthurium UP   Beard-Tongue UPS
Aralia UP   Beauty-berry (callicarpa) UP
Artemisia UPS   Bells of Ireland UP
Artichoke (Cynara cardunculus)   Bitter-Sweet (Celastrus scandens)
 UP   UP
Asparagus UP   Bottle Brush (Calistemon) UP
Aspidistra UP GLYC   Bottle Tree Pods UP

FIG. 68. This arrangement of narcissi and snowdrops in a milk glass container would be suitable for a wedding reception in an Early American type church.

Photo William Arborgast   *Kathryn Davison*

FIG. 69. *Wesley Methodist Church, Palo Alto, Calif.* Pink gladiolus and chrysanthe-mums are silhouetted against the vertically placed New Zealand flax leaves. These are set off to advantage by the warm brown tones in the wooden cross and walls of the church.

Braza (Maxima, Minor) UP
Braziformus (rattlesnake) UP
Brazilian Cedar Pods UP
Buckwheat UP
Burr Oak Acorns UP
Canaigre UPS
Carex UP
Caspia (statice) UPS
Castor Bean Pods UP
Catsclaw UP
Catspaw UP
Cattail UP
Cedar UP
Celosia GLYC
Chinese Houses UP
Chloris Grass UP
Cladium Leaves UP
Clematis PM
Coconut Calyx UP
Coral-Bells (Heuchera) UP
Cotton Calyx UP
Cow Parsnip GLYC
Crape Myrtle Seedpods GLYC
Croton Leaves GLYC
Cryptomeria UPS
Cypress Cones GLYC
Dandelion UP
Dandelion Seed, Leaves UP
Date Diglets UP
Date Palm Seeds, Spathes UP
Deodar Cones (Cedrus deodara)
  UP
Desert Holly (Antriplex
  saltbush) UPS
Devil's Claw (Martyria) UP
Dianthus PM
Dieffenbachia UP

Digger Pine Cones UP
Diosma UP
Dock (Butler, Curley, Fiddle,
  Green, Mexican, Sheep-sorrel,
  Willow) UP
Dogwood (cornus) PM
Douglas Fir Cones UP
Echnops (globe thistle) UP
Elephant Ears UP
Equisetum (horsetail) UP
Eryngium UP
Eucalyptus UP
Dairy Duster (Caeliandra) UP
Fennel UP
Fescue UP
Feverfew UPS
Fiddleneck UP
Flax Seedheads (Linum levesii)
  UP
Forsythia UP
Francoa Seedheads UP
Fungi UP
Ghostwood UPS
Ginkgo UP
Goldenrod UPS
Grape Hyacinth UP
Hackberry UP
Heather UPS
Helichrysum UPS
Hellebore PM
Hollyhock UP
Honey Locust Pods (Gladitsia)
  UP
Hummania UP
Hypericum UPS
Iceland Poppy Seedpods UP
Iris Pods (Foetidisima) UP

FIG. 70. *Stanford University Memorial Church, Stanford, Calif.* Gold-colored leaves of the Modesta Ash, together with purple and green grapes, are arranged on flower standards at either side of this white marble altar. A sheaf of golden wheat decorates the front of the altar. The colors of the plant materials tie harmoniously with the gold-in-crusted mosaics, richly colored paintings, and windows of this Byzantine type interior.

Ironwood Cones   UP
Jacaranda Pods   UP
Jeffery Pine Cones   UP
Joe-Pye Seeds   UP
Larkspur   UPS
Lily Seedpods   UP
Lithospermum   UPS
Lotus Pods (Nelumbium)   UP
Lupin   UPS
Manzanita   UP
Milkweed   UP
Millet   UP
Mimulus Seedpods   UP
Monkshood (Aconitum)   UPS
Mormon Tea (Ephidera)   UP
Mullein   UPS
Nandina   UP
New Zealand Flax   UP
Oleander Pods (Nerium)   UP
Olive   PM
Oriental Poppy   UP
Palmetto   UP
Pansy   PM
Parsnip   UP
Paulownia   PM
Pearly Everlasting (Anaphallis
   margaritsera)   UP
Pelargonium   PM
Pepper Berries (Schinus molle)   UP
Photinia Berries   UP
Pinedrops   UP
Pinyon Pine   UP
Pinyon Pine Cones   UP
Pitcher Plant   UP
Pittosporum Seedpods   UP
Polgonum   UP
Pomegranate   UP
Poppy (Iceland, Oriental Pods and
   Flowers, Shirley)   PM
Primrose Stalks (Oenathera
   deltoides)   UP
Prosopis   UP

Pussy willow   UP
Redbud   UP
Redwood Cones (Sequoia gigantea
   and sempervirens)   UP
Rhododendron Seedpods   UP
Rhubarb   UP
Rose Hips   UP
Royal Poinciana   PM
Salt Cedar   UP
Salvia   UP
Schinus Berries   UP
Scotch Broom   UP
Screwbean   UP
Screwpine   UP
Sea Grape   GLYC
Sea Oats (Uniola paniculata)   UP
Senicco (greyii)   UPS
She Oak (Casuarina)   UP
Silver Tree Seedpods   UPS
Smoke Tree (Parosela spinosa)   UP
Sorghum   UPS
Spoon Plant (Sotol)   UP
Spruce Cones   UP
Staff-flower (Carthamus
   tinctorius)   UPS
Statice (Timonium)   UP
Stercula Pods   UP
Succulents (Echiveria, Grapopla-
   lum, Houseleeks, Sedum)   UP
Sugar Cane Stalks   UP
Sugar Pine Cones (Pinus
   lambertiana)   UP
Sunflower   UP
Sweet Gum Balls (Liquidambar
   styraciflua)   UP
Tamarack Cones (Pinus
   contorta)   UP
Tamarix   UPS
Teasel (Dipsucus)   UP
Thread Plant   UP
Veronica   UPS
Washingtonia (Fan palm)   UP

Yarrow UP
Yerba Mansa (Cinemopsis
  california) UPS
Yucca UP

Hawaiian Material

Baby Woodrose (Argyreia
  nervosa) UP
Bamboo Sheaths UP
Christmas Berry (Schinus terebinthi-
  folius) UP
Elephant Ears (Enterelibium cyclo-
  carpum) UP
Hawaiian Fernwood (for
  bases) UP

Hawaiian Palm Sheaths UP
Koa Haole Mimosa, Leucaena
  glauca) UP
Lipstick Pods (Bixa orellana) UP
Palm Boat (for container) UP
Sea Grape Leaves (Coccolaba
  uvifera) UP
Tulip Tree Pods (Spathodea
  campanulata) UP (Spray with
  lacquer)
Volcanic Grass UP
Wili Wili (Adenatheria
  pavonia) UP
Woodrose (Ipomea tuberosa
  linneaus) UP

K. SUITABLE FOR CORSAGES

Single Pierce Method

  Bachelor Button
  Carnation
  Dianthus
  Fuchsia
  Rose
  Sweet William

Weak Calyx

  Begonia, tuberous
  Camellia
  Gardenia

Hook Method

  Aster
  Chrysanthemum
  Daisy
  Gaillardia
  Lily
  Rheum
  Scabiosa
  Tuberose
  Tulip Tree sp.
  Zinnia

Clutch or Splint Method

  Agapanthus
  Amaryllis
  Anthurium
  Azalea
  Christmas Rose
  Crocus
  Cyclamen
  Daffodil
  Day Lily
  Dendrobium
  Epidendrum
  Epiphyllum
  Geranium
  Gerbera
  Gladiolus florets
  Hellebore
  Hibiscus
  Hollyhock
  Hyacinth
  Iris
  Petunia
  Phalenopsis (orchid)
  Poppy (Iceland)
  Primrose

Clutch or Splint Method (Cont.)

  Scilla
  Tigridia
  Tulip
  Watsonia florets

Hairpin Method

  Calendula
  Chrysanthemum
  Clematis
  Dahlia
  Daisy (large)
  Marguerite

Peony
Poinsettia

Requiring Cotton-Wrapped
Stem Before Wiring

  Ageratum
  Althea
  Azalea
  Babys-breath (Gypsophila)
  Bouvardia
  Bridal wreath (Spirea)
  Cherry (flowering)
  Clematis

VII. Instructions for Making a Color Wheel

HOW TO MAKE YOUR OWN COLOR WHEEL
WITH PIGMENT WATER COLORS

Materials Needed

1. Two sheets 9 x 22 inches of black railroad board for mounting wheel
2. Pad of water-color paper 9 x 11 inches, or Cambridge drawing paper. (About 150 two-by-two-inch squares will be needed.)
3. Rubber cement for pasting down colors.
4. Ruler.
5. Scissors.
6. Compass.
7. Medicine dropper.
8. Muffin pan or other receptacle for mixing colors and holding water.
9. Lintless cloths for drying and wiping brushes.
10. Two pint jars for holding water.
11. White ink for marking colors.
12. Water-color paints.
    Method No. 1—Transparent Grumbacher Brilliant Water Colors.
    Method No. 2—Opaque paint (poster paints).
13. Three brushes (usually included in paintbox) Sizes 7, 8, 9.
14. Color chart for comparing colors (see notes).
15. Plastic groundcloth 56 inches square to cover and protect table.
16. Blotters to touch overfilled brushes.

Good lighting is essential. At night, work under daylight bulbs or daylight-corrected fluorescent bulbs. In daylight hours work near north window, light coming over left shoulder.

Method No. 1—Using Transparent Water Colors

1. Choose Grumbacher Color Wheel to follow in painting. Make a 12-hue wheel.

199

2. Cut 150 two-by-two-inch squares from drawing paper. Use rough side for painting surface. Use Cambridge water-color paper.
3. Wet 3 primary paint tabs in box so that the colors may be mixed more easily.
4. Mix each hue in turn in muffin tin with a few drops of water from medicine dropper.
5. Stir gently—avoid making bubbles. Approximate each primary with that of wheel.
6. Lift sufficient paint with wet brush from muffin tin to cover square. It should be mixed thin enough so that the desired richness and intensity of hue coincides with that of hue on wheel, but should be of a consistency that will dry without making black streaks. The effect of brightness and transparency is the result of light reflected from the surface of the paper. The pigment acts as a filter and allows only certain light rays to pass through it.

The paint should be wet enough to flow onto the square of paper and form an even surface. Hold paper at a 5- to 10-degree angle. Work quickly from left to right. Allow each stroke to bleed into next stroke.

While the paper is still damp, slightly flatten brush and with light, even strokes, brush from top of square downward, holding brush parallel to strokes. Overlap each stroke until paint is evenly distributed. If bubbles have formed, suck them up with brush that has been touched to blotter. Do no brushing after surface of paper has dried.

Care of Brushes. Each brush should be carefully washed with soap and water, dried, and placed in a dry glass with bristles pointing skyward.

Use no white paint to approximate hues of color chart. White would change value of hue. By adding water one finds more light is reflected through pigment from paper, giving much the same effect as adding white pigment.

Continue to make squares until you are satisfied with smoothness of work and good color.

At first the colors will look too shiny, but will flatten when dry.

Continue with secondary colors. Keep brushes scrupulously clean between paintings of each hue.

Do not use secondary colors in box but mix them to approximate those of color wheel. In this way the student learns basic mixtures. Mix:

Red + yellow = orange
Yellow + blue = green
Blue + red = violet

When the primaries and secondaries are in place on the wheel they are known as standard colors. They are the strength of color visible on the spectral band. Continue to make a number of these hues until you are satisfied as to their trueness to the chart you are trying to approximate.

Tertiary or intermediate colors are combinations of secondary and primary colors. They are more tricky to mix because three colors are involved in their admixture. They are, however, subtle colors and are beautiful in arrangements when used together.

Tertiary

Red + orange = R O
Yellow + orange = Y O
Yellow + green = Y G
Blue + green = B G
Blue + violet = B V
Red + violet = R V

You now have twelve hues ready for the color circle. If more are required you continue to mix intermediate colors in multiples of six.

After squares are dry, turn them over and, with compass set ¾ inch, make a circle on center of each square. Cut out along circle. Lay aside to mount on wheel with rubber cement.

With compass set at 3 inches draw a circumference on center of black railroad board (9 x 12 inches).

Visualize clock face.

With compass still set at 3 inches, at exact top of circumference, set point of compass and strike arcs around circumference, at two o'clock, four, six, eight, ten, and twelve. Now reverse procedure and strike arcs around circumference counterclockwise at each hour mentioned above. The circumference will have six equal divisions.

Place primaries (see Fig. 19):
yellow at 12 o'clock
red at 4 o'clock
blue at 8 o'clock
Next place secondaries:
orange at 2 o'clock
violet at 6 o'clock
green at 10 o'clock
Then place tertiaries:
yellow-orange at 1 o'clock
red-orange at 3 o'clock
red-violet at 5 o'clock
blue-violet at 7 o'clock
blue-green at 9 o'clock
yellow-green at 11 o'clock

Method No. 2—Using Opaque Water-Color Paints

Proceed as in Method No. 1. Opaque water-color paints are duller than transparent paint. They are known as poster paints, are soluble in water, and will cover any paper with an opaque coating.

When one becomes proficient in the use of opaque paints one may make a value chart. By including white and black pigments, and by varying the value of each hue from light to dark, one may become familiar with gradations. Eventually one will have made his own color chart as a permanent guide for future flower-arrangement plans.

Standard Materials to Select from in Making Color Wheel and Chart

Papers

Strathmore
Grumbacher
Bainbridge
  Watman (English)
  d'Arches (French)
  Fabriano (Italian)

Brushes

Winsor & Newton
Grumbacher
Delta

Colors (Oil or Water-Color Paints)

Winsor & Newton
  Grumbacher (Schminke)
  Permanent Pigments
  Devoe
  Prang

Color Wheels

Cheskin
Grumbacher
Munsell
Prang
Oswald

VIII. Liturgical Church Calendar

Date	Day or Season	Symbolic Meaning	Vestment Color	Decorations
4 Sundays preceding Christmas	Advent	Anticipation	Violet	Advent Wreath, no flowers
Third Sunday of Advent	Gaudete Sunday		Rose	Roses and lilies
Dec. 21	St. Thomas Apostle		Red	No flowers
Dec. 24	Eve of Nativity		White	Flowers, greens, and candles
Dec. 25	Christmas		White	Red, green, gold, silver, and pastel flowers, also greens and candles
Dec. 26	St. Stephen		Red	Red flowers to simulate flame
Dec. 27	St. John, Evangelist		White	White flowers
Dec. 28	Holy Innocents		Red, if Sunday; violet, if weekday	Red roses
Jan. 1	Circumcision or Holy Name of Jesus		White	Red roses
Jan. 6	Epiphany and its octave	Manifestation, 3 crowns	White	Crèche, flowers, greens
Jan. 25	Conversion of St. Paul and St. Peter		Red or White	
Feb. 2	Purification of the Blessed Virgin Mary		White	Flowers such as lilies and roses
Feb. 1	Candlemas	Blessing of candles	Violet	Flowers also decorated with candles
Feb. 24	St. Matthias, Apostle	Commemoration of martyrdom	Red	

MOVABLE FEASTS PRECEDING EASTER AND FOLLOWING EASTER

Date	Day or Season	Symbolic Meaning	Vestment Color	Decorations
	Septuagesima, 3 Sundays before Lent		Green	No flowers. Decorated with candles
	Sexagesima, 2 Sundays before Lent		Green	No flowers. Decorated with candles
	Quinquagesima, the Sunday before Lent		Green	No flowers. Decorated with candles
	Shrove Tuesday, day before Ash Wednesday		Green	No flowers. Decorated with candles
	Ash Wednesday, beginning of Lent		Violet	
4th Sunday of Lent	Laetare Sunday	Golden rose	Rose	
Mar. 25	Annunciation	Lily	White	White flowers
	Passion Sunday	Crucifix		Cross is veiled in violet
	Palm Sunday, Sunday preceding Easter	Palms	Violet	Palms and olive branches may be used
	Maundy Thursday of Holy Week		White	Many flowers to represent garden. Altar is stripped
	Good Friday	Cross	Black	No flowers. After mass High Altar stripped. Flowers on altar of repose
	Holy Saturday		White	Flowers

FLOWER CHURCH CALENDAR

Date	Day or Season	Symbolic Meaning	Vestment Color	Decorations
	Easter	Cross	White	Many flowers, especially lilies
April 25	St. Mark the Evangelist		Violet or red	No flowers
May 1	St. Philip and St. James		Red	
	The Ascension, 40 days after Easter		White	White flowers
	Whitsunday or Pentecost, 50 days after Easter	Dove	Red	Red flowers
	Holy Trinity, First Sunday after Pentecost	Three circles	White for Sunday; green for season	Flowers
June 11	St. Barnabas		Red	Flowers
June 24	Nativity of St. John the Baptist		White	Flowers
June 29	St. Peter the Apostle		Red	Flowers
July 2	Visitation		White	Flowers
July 25	St. James and St. Christopher		Red	Flowers
Aug. 1	St. Peter and St. Paul		White	Flowers
Aug. 6	Transfiguration		White	Flowers
Aug. 15	Assumption		White	Flowers
Aug. 24	St. Bartholomew		Red	Flowers
Sept. 21	St. Matthew, Evangelist		Red	Flowers
Sept. 29	St. Michael and All Angels		White	Flowers
Oct. 18	St. Luke, Evangelist		Red	Flowers
Oct. 28	St. Simon and St. Jude, Apostles		Red	Flowers
Nov. 1	All Saints Day		White	Flowers
Nov. 30	St. Andrew, Apostle		Red	Flowers

The colors yellow and blue are strictly forbidden in vestments when decorating the High Altar. Nor may the color gold be used, except when the frontal is cloth of gold or when special ecclesiastical privilege is granted for a certain time. Cloth of silver may be used in place of white vestments, and gold cloth may be used instead of red, white, or green (Catholic).

Violet is used for vigils, Rogation Days, penitential days and Ember Days, except for Pentecost week.

Baptism	White
Confirmation	White
Ordination	White
Wedding	White
Child's funeral	White
Adult funeral	Black
Requiem function	Black

Glossary

Abstract design. Does not follow nature.

Accessory. Anything other than plant material, container, and base, included in an arrangement.

Advent. Begins with fourth Sunday preceding Christmas; a time of preparation for Christ's coming.

Apostolic Constitution. Documents compiled at Antioch in the 4th century, describing church practices of the time.

Apse. Semicircular construction at opposite end of church's entrance; place where altar is set.

Ash Wednesday. Beginning of Lent.

Baldacchino or ciborium. A canopy, mark of honor, supported above altar.

Balsam. Sweet-smelling resin from certain trees and plants, blessed and used in chrism.

Balustrade. Usually a low fence or rail separating sanctuary from church proper.

Blessing new fire. Performed on Holy Saturday evening preceding Easter, when Paschal Candle is lighted.

Buttress. Masonry support to relieve tension from downward and outward thrust of heavy ceiling.

Cantilever. Construction bearing horizontal weight of building.

Ceramics. Refers to containers and accessories usually made of pottery.

Ceremonial of bishops. Book containing ceremonial procedure for cathedrals or collegiate churches.

Chancel. Part of church, elevated, between nave and sanctuary.

Chevet. French term for apse, where side chapels are part of church.

Classic. Referring to culture of ancient Greece.

Clerestory window. Window placed high in nave, above side aisles.

Conventionalized design. Stylized type of applied design.

Corporal. Square piece of linen placed on altar under objects holding Holy Eucharist.

Decorative. Applied decoration.

Depth. Occupied space of plant material from front to back in an arrangement; also measurement downward in container.

Design. Planned arrangement of parts.

Distinction. Exceptional proficiency in composing an arrangement, calling forth immediate response in viewer.

Distortion. Twisting or manipulating plant materials into unnatural shapes.

Dorsal. A cloth hanging placed back of and above altar.

Dynamic. Conveying a feeling of movement.

Dynamic symmetry. Art reduced to mathematical science.

Epistle side of altar. Left side of altar when facing it from nave.

Façade. Front elevation of building.

Faience. Glazed pottery.

Fan vaulting. Ribs radiating from a point on a ceiling.

Flamboyant. Flame-shaped applied decoration.

Flying buttress. Masonry-supported arch that counteracts lateral thrust of weight from roof.

Formal. Symmetrical arrangement.

Fresco painting. Pigment applied in design to wet plaster.

Gaudete. Third Sunday in Advent; to mark period showing joy, Christ's birth is near.

Geometric design. Natural objects are reduced to geometric figures.

Greek cross. Arms of cross are of equal length and cross each other in exact center to form right angles.

Gregorian water. Water to which salt, ashes, and wine have been added and the whole blessed.

Holy Saturday. Day before Easter, which commemorates the burial of Jesus. In late afternoon, the Paschal Candle is lighted.

Holy Week. Week preceding Easter, beginning Monday following Palm Sunday.

Icon. Portrait of a sacred image.

Laetare Sunday. Fourth Sunday in Lent. Vestments are rose colored. In ancient times, the Pope blessed a golden rose.

Lent. Forty days preceding Easter, beginning on Ash Wednesday.

Lunette. Three-dimensional design of half-moon or crescent.

Memorial Rituum. Book setting forth certain ecclesiastical directives for a parish church.

Motif. Distinct shape and form of design.

Name of Jesus (Holy). Sunday between January 1 and January 6.

Narthex. Porch or entrance to church.

Nave. Main part of church.

Octave. Seven-day period following a solemnity.

Originality. Unusual plant material, container, or accessory, arranged in an unusual way.

Paschal time. Period of time following Easter and continuing until Saturday after Pentecost.

Precious Blood (feast day). July 1.

Relief. Sculptured figures on walls or plaques. In low (or *bas*) relief, only half of figure shows; in high relief, figure is rounded. Sunken relief is known as *intaglio*.

Reredos. Decorated wall or screen behind and above altar.

Retable. Shelf back of altar.

Ribs. Stone arches which form framework of many cathedrals.

Rococo. Predominantly curvilinear over-ornamentation, prevalent in French art during time of Louis XV (18th century).

Rubrics. Book of rules which contain liturgical ceremony of worship.

Style. Typical expression in the arts of a particular period.

Symbolic. Explained by a symbol rather than by direct representation of an object.

Tactile. Surface quality appealing to sense of touch.

Tension. Force that develops where plants spring from earth. Also outward force exerted by weight from above and sides.

Three-dimensional. Having height (or length), breadth and thickness. Objects in space.

Tracery. Stone, wooden, metal, or marble mullions used on Gothic cathedral windows or woodwork.

Two-dimensional. Having height (or length) and width.

Unity. The quality in an arrangement whereby each element is in agreement, to effect a harmonious whole. Oneness.

Vaults. Arched ceilings in churches.

Bibliography

Abrams, Leroy: "Illustrated Flora of the Pacific States," Stanford, California, Stanford University Press, 1940.

Berrale, Julia S.: "A History of Flower Arrangement," New York, Studio-Crowell, 1953.

Bowers, Nathan A.: "Cone-Bearing Trees of the Pacific Coast," New York, McGraw-Hill, 1942.

Chiskin, Louis: "How to Tune Color to Your Home," New York, Macmillan, 1954.

Conway, J. Gregory: "Conway's Encyclopedia of Flower Arrangement," New York, Alfred A. Knopf, 1957.

Cyphers, Emma Hodkinson: "Design and Depth," New York, Hearthside Press, 1958.

Derieux, Mary, and Stevenson, Isabella: "Interior Decoration," New York, Greystone Press, 1951.

Dow, Arthur W.: "Composition," New York, Country Life Press, 1913.

Drier, Katherine: "Three Lectures on Modern Art," New York, Philosophical Library, 1948.

Drummond, Hazel: "Corsages with Garden Flowers," New York, Macmillan, 1935.

Emerson, Sybie: "Design," Scranton, International Text Book Co., 1953.

Faulkner, R., Ziegfield, E., and Hill, G.: "Art Today" New York, Henry Holt, 1941.

Fletcher, Sir Banister: "A History of Architecture," London, B. T. Botsford, Ltd., 1928.

Gardner, Helen: "Art Through the Ages," New York, Harcourt, Brace, 1948.

Germaine, Ina M.: "Design for Decoration," New York, McBride, 1946.

Gihr, Rev. Dr. Nicholas: "The Holy Sacrifice of the Mass" (translated from the German), St. Louis, Mo., B. Herder Book Co., 1949.

Gilbert, K. C., and Kuhn, H.: "A History of Esthetics," Bloomington, Indiana, University of Indiana Press, 1953.

Goldstein, Harriet, and Goldstein, Vetta: "Art in Everyday Life," New York, Macmillan, 1925.

Golson, Rae L.: "Contemporary Flower Arrangement," New York, Hearthside Press, 1955.

Groves, Maitland: "The Art of Color and Design," New York, McGraw-Hill, n.d.

Guptill, Arthur: "Color in Sketching and Rendering," New York, Reinhold, 1935.

Hayes, Naida Gilmore: "Landscape Flower Arrangements," Studio-Crowell, New York and London, 1953.

Hayes, William C.: "The Scepter of Egypt," New York, Harper, 1953.

Hitchcock, A. S.: "Manual of the Grasses of the United States," Washington, D.C., U.S., Dept. of Agriculture Miscell. Pub. No. 200, Government Printing Office, 1935.

Hole, Christina: "Christmas and Its Customs," New York, Barrows, 1958.

Jepson, Willis Linn: "Flowering Plants of California," Berkeley and Los Angeles, University of California Press, 1951.

Kittel, Mary Badham: "Easy Ways to Good Flower Arrangement," New York, Studio-Crowell, 1957.

Koehn, Alfred: "Japanese Classical Flower Arrangement," Rutland, Vt., and Tokyo, Japan, Charles E. Tuttle Co., 1951.

Monks, James L.: "Great Catholic Festivals," New York, Harry Schuman, Inc., 1957.

Obata, Mme. Chuira: "Japanese Flower Arrangement," Berkeley, California, University of California Press, n.d.

Obata, Haruko: "An Illustrated Handbook of Japanese Flower Arrangement," Berkeley, California, University of California Press, 1940.

O'Connell, J. B. (S.J.): "The Celebration of the Mass," Milwaukee, Wisconsin, Bruce Publishing Co., 1956.

Rister, Dorothy W.: "Design for Flower Arrangers," Princeton, New Jersey, Van Nostrand, 1959.

Rockwell, F. F., and Grayson, Esther: "The Complete Book of Flower Arrangement," New York, American Garden Guild and Doubleday, 1947.

Scott, M. Gladys: "Analysis of Human Motion," New York, F. S. Crofts, n.d.

Sofu, Teshigahara: "Coloured Pictures of Representative Flower Arrangements by Sofu," Tokyo, Japan, The Ryufusha Publishing Co., Ltd., 1951.

Stelle, Anita: "Seven Keys to Distinction in Flower Arrangement," New York, Hearthside Press, 1957.

Stoltz, Mrs. Raymond Russ: "Flower Show Ribbon-Winning Arrangements," New York, Scribner's, 1958.

Taubes, Frederick: "Pictorial Composition and the Art of Drawing," New York, Dodd, Mead, 1949.

Underwood, Raye Miller: "The Complete Book of Dried Arrangements," New York, Barrows, 1952.

Van Rensselaer, Elinor: "Decorating with Pods and Cones," Princeton, New Jersey, Van Nostrand, 1957.

Waters, Clara Erskine Clement: "A Handbook of Christian Symbols and Stories of the Saints," Houghton Mifflin Co., New York, 1886.

Wilson, Albert: "Gardeners All," Palo Alto, California, Albert Wilson Publishing Co., 1953.

Wilson, Adelaide: "Color in Flower Arrangement," New York, Barrows, 1954.

——: "Flower Arranging for Churches," New York, 1952.

Wilson, Helen Van Pelt: "The Joy of Flower Arranging," New York, Barrows, 1951.

——: "Perennials Preferred," New York, Barrows, 1945.

Index

(Page numbers in *italics* refer to illustrations)

215